MY ITALY STORY and
LONG GONE DADDY

"Author Joseph Gallo delivers the kind of emotional knockout we seldom get from more famous playwrights in bigger plays."

- Gannett Newspapers

MY ITALY STORY and LONG GONE DADDY

Two Plays by Joseph Gallo

Sordelet Ink/Chicago

Two Plays: My Italy Story and Long Gone Daddy
Copyright @ 2016 by Joseph Gallo

My Italy Story was originally produced by Penguin Repertory Company – Joe Brancato, Artistic Director; Andrew M. Horn, Executive Director – in Stony Point, NY.

Long Gone Daddy was developed in All For One's SoloLab 2014 at the Paradise Factory Theatre in New York City.

No part of this book may be reproduced in any form or by any means, electronic or mechanical, including photocopying or recording, or by an information storage and retrieval system, without permission in writing from the author.

Professionals and amateurs are hereby warned that this material being fully protected under the Copyright Laws of the United States of America and all other countries of the Berne and Universal Copyright Conventions, is subject to a royalty. All rights including, but not limited to, professional, amateur, recording, motion picture, recitation, lecturing, public reading, radio and television broadcasting, podcasts, and websites, and the rights of translation into foreign languages are expressly reserved.

Library of Congress Cataloging-in-Publication Data
Gallo, Joseph
Two Plays: My Italy Story and Long Gone Daddy/Joseph Gallo. – 1st ed.
p. cm.
I. Title

ISBN 13: 978-1-944540-18-0
ISBN 10: 1-944540-18-0

Book Design: Michael Blaskewicz
Author Photo: Michael O'Brien
Cover Photo: Dairen Coto

Sordelet Ink, July 2016
First Edition

CONTENTS

Preface	vii
Acknowledgments	ix
My Italy Story	1
Long Gone Daddy	49
Afterward	103

PREFACE

My Mother (Mom, Blanche, Bronislava) is/was the best storyteller I know. As an old-school, stay-at-home housewife, she would while away the days by spinning weekly yarns to her many girlfriends over the telephone – Yanyah Zaniewska, Trudy with a "Y", Eleanor from Across the Street, etc., etc. She would individually tell them the story of her day, but with each telling she would change the details, improving the story as she went along. A little expansion here, an embellishment there. A joke, perhaps. A natural born editor, she could and would cut with impunity, until a mundane task like doing the laundry could turn into a legend worthy of Flannery O' Connor.

     Eavesdropping on those tales is where my education as a storyteller began.

ACKNOWLEDGMENTS

I would like to extend a humble thank you to the following people and organizations who helped to make these two plays possible.

My Italy Story – Spalding Gray, Chazz Palminteri, Louie Gallo, Gerardo Gallo, Jimmy Gallo, Donna Coney Island, Ken Friedland, The Waterfront Ensemble (Hoboken), Nancy Robillard, Steve Dennis, Joe Brancato, Andrew M. Horn, Penguin Rep, DJ Silky, Danny Mastrogiorgio, Jere Couture, Evangeline Morphos, Mara Gibbs, Ron Gwiazda, 12 Miles West, Lenny Bart, Frank Licato, Vincent Sagona, Joe Mancuso, Chris O'Connor and Mile Square Theatre, Matt Lawler, Richie Call, and Tom Pelphrey.

Long Gone Daddy – Sarah Weber Gallo, Olivia Gallo, Ohio University, Armin Brott, The Moth, Michael O'Brien, Chris Butler, The Farm (John Kaplan, Robert Lyons, Ron Dobson, Steven Haworth), Jose Suarez, Erich Jungwirth, Artistic New Directions, Janice Goldberg, Kristine Niven, David Marx, Robin A. Paterson, Shetler Studios, The Actors Studio, Nicole Haran, Nelson Avidon, Michael Wolk, All For One, Jean-Michele Gregory, Chris O'Connor and Mile Square Theatre (again), Andrew Baldwin, Elizabeth DiCandilo, Zabrina Stoffel, everyone who hosted a Salon, Jeanne and Bruce Lubin, Dairen Coto, Rick Sordelet, David Blixt, and especially Michael Blaskewicz (who put the M in MJ).

MY ITALY STORY

For Alfred, Blanche, Nancy, and the entire Gallo family

PRODUCTION HISTORY

My Italy Story opened Off-Broadway at the 47th Street Theatre in New York City on April 1, 1997, with:

    THOMAS DAGATO   Daniel Mastrogiorgio

The production was directed by Joe Brancato; scenic design by Jeff Cowie; lighting design by Jeff Nellis; sound design by Johnna Doty; and the production stage manager was Kathleen J. Dooner. It was produced by Evangeline Morphos, Mara Gibbs, and Gary Shaffer.

My Italy Story received a revival at Mile Square Theatre in Hoboken, NJ, which opened on June 17, 2009, with:

    THOMAS DAGATO   Tom Pelphrey

The production was directed by Matthew Lawler; set design by Jasmine Vogue Pai; lighting design by Laura Cornish; costume design by Caitlin J. Doukas; sound design by Matthew Sherwin; projection design by Amith Chandrashaker; and the production stage manager was Christopher Rinaldi. It was produced by Chris O' Connor, Artistic Director, Mile Square Theatre.

ACT ONE

Dreams and Visions of My Grandmother

1.

Lights up on THOMAS DAGATO, late 20s, wearing a suit and tie.

My story starts on a summer night.
   Hoboken.
   3 a.m.

   I sleep in the fetal position, my hand inside my pillow case, a blue sheet over my body. No matter how hot it gets, I have to cover myself with, at least, a sheet. The window in my room is open there is no breeze.
   And then...I feel it...
   There's a presence in my room. I know that it's there.
I know that it's something I can't avoid.
   I turn...

   On top of my dresser I see my Grandmother who has been dead for more than 18 years. She looks exactly as I last remember her, dressed in widow black. She's silhouetted by these white, swirling shadows.
   I scream, "AHHH!"
   A second later The Woman In The Apartment Upstairs From Mine screams, "AHHH!"
   What was that?

2.

The next morning, I'm at work preparing for a blue line meeting with a client. I'm an account executive. It's my fourth and hopefully my final presentation of a new brochure. I'm getting ready to walk out the door, and just as I zip up my portfolio the office secretary says, "There's an important call on line one."

It's my Brother-In-Law.

He says, "It's over."

I say, "What's over?"

He says, "Your Sister had the Baby. You're an uncle."

"Boy or girl?"

"You know...," he says. "...after the Baby came out the nurse just took it away. I forgot to ask!"

3.

In a South Jersey hospital, my little Sister sits in bed surrounded by flowers, family, friends, holding her Baby *boy*. She tells us all about her experience giving birth. How when her water broke, she'd thought she'd wet the bed. How my Brother-In-Law took a short cut to the hospital, and got lost. How she'd spent 13 hours in labor. Then my Mother tells the story of when she gave birth to my Sister.

And I say, "What about me?"

My Mother says, "Thomas, please. We're not talkin' about you. We're talkin' about your Sister. When you have kids, we'll talk about you."

Then, she just turns away, back to my Sister...

Later, on the ride home, she says, "Do you think I favor your Sister over you? Don't ever think I love your Sister more than you. I don't play favorites. I love both of you the same."

I say, "Mom, what are you talking about?"

And she says, "Never mind. It's just... It's a mother thing. That's all."

4.

I visit my Sister again in the hospital, and this time she says, "I want you to be the Godfather of the Baby."

It's an honor.

There's an old Italian saying that, "The world is so hard a child must have two fathers to look after him, and that's why they have godfathers."

Then my Sister adds, "And are you still with `off-again, Anna-again'?"

My ex-girlfriend's nickname was "off-again, Anna-again." Her real name was Anna, but we had broken up so many times that everyone just called her "off-again, Anna-again."

I say, "We're off-again. Why?"

"Because after the christening there's gonna be a party."

I say, "Great. Whose invited?"

She says, "Everybody. All the relatives."

"All the relatives?"

She says, "Yup. Every single one."

I say, "Do you think that's a good idea?"

She says, "Yeah. Why not?"

I say, "Because there are people in our family who don't talk to each other. They don't like each other. You want them at your party?"

She says, "Look, Thomas... Daddy's dead. The Baby's never gonna know who he was. He should, at least, know Daddy's brothers and sisters. Doncha think?"

I try and remember the last time all my relatives were in the same room together. I can't. There are factions of my Father's side of the family who haven't spoken to each other in more than 18 years. My Father had five brothers, and two sisters, that's eight siblings, plus 16 nieces and nephews.

One fight divided them all.

The central figures in the argument were my Uncle Rudy and my Aunt Florence. It was primarily my uncle versus my aunt, brother against sister. The rest of the relatives either aligned themselves with my Uncle Rudy, or like my father, remained neutral, neutral meaning not siding with my Uncle Rudy, but not speaking to my Aunt Florence, either.

It all started when my Grandmother passed away. What happened? I'm not sure... I was only 11 years old. But I do know that when my Grandmother died, she left no will. And I remember an argument at my aunt's house. Everyone was at the kitchen table, yelling back and forth, standing, red faced, spitting, crying, flailing their hands, cursing, pointing fingers. My Uncle Rudy accused my Aunt Florence of going into my Grandmother's house and stealing things, jewelry, etc. My Aunt Florence accused my Uncle Rudy of not properly dividing the money and house my Grandmother had left behind. And the argument just roared on with accusations whirling around the room, coming to a stop, and whirling around again, until finally my Father banged his fists down on the kitchen table, and screamed, "*Stai-zito! Stai-zito!*"

Also seated at the table was my Cousin Gerardo, who was 17, visiting from Italy, from Vallata, my Grandfather's village. He didn't speak English. As the fight swirled around us, I looked at him, and he made this face that asked, "What is going on?"

I never found out.

In passing years, my Father died of a heart attack, and the gap between the family...just grew. Whenever I asked my Mother about the argument she gave me answers like, "It's an old fight. Why bring it up? It's over. It's been so blown out of proportion that I don't think anyone knows what happened anymore."

5.

The christening party takes place in my Sister's backyard. By mid-afternoon, it's a hundred degrees...and nobody's there. My Sister is freaking out!
And then...
My cousin Louie appears at the gate. My Father's nephew. "Louie!"
My Sister runs over to give him a kiss. My Mother runs over to give him a kiss. I run over to shake his hand, and he grabs the back of my head, and says, "What are you too old to kiss your cousin!" Then he plants one right on my lips, steps back, and says, "Where's the baby?"
My Sister says, "He's in the house. He's asleep."
He says, "Wake him up! We gotta wake him up! We don't want him to forget this!"
He starts for the house. My Sister cuts him off. He puts on a fake struggle. "No! No! We gotta wake him up! We gotta wake him up!" And he keeps pushing it, and pushing it, until he doubles over, laughing.

Louie is my absolute favorite. When he was younger, he played drums in a rock and roll band, and drove around in a `72 Pontiac convertible, blue with white interior. Now he drives a delivery truck. He's the family cut-up. He's wearing a loud, print shirt and double knit pants. In fact, he's been wearing the same clothes like 20 years.

I say, "Louie, when did you get that shirt 1974?"
He says, "No. This is new. I got it in the 80's."

Louie pops his first beer just as a caravan of relatives drives up to the front of the house. Aunts. Friends of the family who called themselves aunts. Cousins. Second cousins. My Uncle Rudy...

My Uncle Rudy rarely leaves the house. He is famous for plopping himself down in one spot, and staying there for hours at a time. He's a retired Teamster. He has faded tattoos on both of his arms that now look like huge black and blue marks. He's something out of the movie ON THE WATERFRONT. He's... And I guess there's no nice way to say this... He's fat. I mean when he sits down his chair actually disappears. He never married, and until my Grandmother died, had spent his entire adult life living in rented rooms. He is the absolute authority on every and any subject, and whenever he talked to you, he constantly tapped your arm to make sure you were listening. He hasn't been to a family outing in years, and the first words out of his mouth..., "Tommy! Why ya wanna live in Hoboken? Huh? Grandpa spends his whole life workin' to get the family outta Hoboken, and what do you do? You move right back!"

6.

Hours later.
Louie yells at me across the yard, "Tommy... I'll have one if you have one."

"I'll have one if you have one..." It was a favorite party time saying between Louie and my Father. One of them would yell out, "I'll have one if you have one." Then the other would yell, "I'll have one if you have one," and they'd just keep repeating it all the way to the bar, where they'd do shots of Canadian Club or Seagram's 7. It became such a ritual, that when my Father died, Louie placed two shot glasses in his coffin...for when they got to the other side.

"I'll have one if you have one," Louie says.
I say, "I'll have one if you have one."
And we walk over to the bar...and do a shot.

Then Louie says, "Tommy... C'mon, let's talk." He throws an arm around my shoulder, scoops my Mother up in his other arm, and the three of us make our way out to the back of the yard.
"Look at this," Louie says. "This is great. Almost everybody's here..."
I say, "What do you mean `almost'?"
He says, "Cousin Eugene didn't come. His mother didn't come - Aunt Florence."
I tell him that we didn't expect Aunt Florence, or Eugene to come. That no one had talked to them since the split. I tell him that Eugene did send a card though, and that was something.
"Yeah...yeah...," Louie says. "Eugene and I usta be best friends. When we were kids we usta play stickball together, sneak cigarettes down the corner. I was at his house every day, sleepin' over... We were together all the time. And now...now...I haven't seen him since Grandma died. Hey, do you remember how we usta go over Grandma's house every single Sunday? The entire family. Uncle Rudy. Aunt Florence. Everybody talkin', tellin' stories, laughin'. Remember that?"

As Louie talks, I remember my own version of Sundays at Grandma's. Mine starts with an image of Grandma in the kitchen, cooking. She's dressed like a gypsy. She always dressed like a gypsy. And she had the softest voice. I can still hear her at the screen door, calling my name. I'd be playing with my cousins beneath the fig trees, or running around the yard with Rip, the family dog, who was part German Shepard, part wolf, and at the sound of her voice, I would just freeze as if playing Statues. "Tomas! Tomas!" For this was my call to duty. For I was my Grandmother's official spaghetti taster.

I'd sprint into the house, looking at my feet, always looking at my feet, out of fear of possibly stepping on one of my Grandfather's pet turtles. They roamed freely around the house, six of them. My Grandfather printed numbers on their backs with white paint so he could tell them apart. I'd hop over turtle number two, put on the brakes, skid into the kitchen, and come to a stop right in front of the stove, where my Grandmother stood waiting, a wooden spoon in her hand, one or two noodles twisted around the neck.

She'd say, "Be careful now. It's hot. You blow on it and tell me whatcha think."

I loved my Grandmother's pasta so much that she would give me a spaghetti sandwich for the ride home, which I would save, and bring to school the following day, and at lunch I'd have to sit by myself, because the other kids would be like, "Eooo! What are you eating? Brains?"

At dinner, we would sit in the kitchen at two picnic tables lined end-to-end, sometimes 20, 25 people. And it was there that I would hear the telling and the retelling of our family myths, and even though I heard the same stories repeated over and over again, I would sit and listen to the tales as if hearing them for the first time. It was one of the traditions of the Sunday gathering, second only to the moment when Grandpa would pour each of us a glass of his homemade wine, which he made right in the cellar of the house.

Grandpa used to say that Sunday was the most important day of the week, because it was the only time that the entire family was together.

Back in the yard, Louie says, "*La via vecchia.* The old way was better."

My Mother says, "It's a shame what happens to families... How they stop talkin' to each other. But what are ya gonna do? People fight. They divorce. They move away. That's life... After my husband died...your side of the family...," and she points at Louie, "...stopped comin' around the house. No phone calls, either. Nothin'. We were married for 36 years. You figure that out."

I say, "Louie, why don't you just give Eugene a call?"

He says, "What? And go against Uncle Rudy? If he found out, you know how much trouble he'd cause? He'd kick me outta the family, same as Eugene. It's ridiculous... We havta get the family back together, Tommy. Every body. Otherwise, the family's never gonna be the same. And Uncle Rudy's never gonna speak to Aunt Florence and Cousin Eugene again."

I say, "How? We tried inviting everyone."

"I dunno how," Loue says. "But we'll find a way. Just promise me."

I say, "Promise what?"

He says, "Promise me we'll get the family back together."

The Louie who waits for my response is not the Louie I'm use to - the family cut-up. No. The Louie who waits for my response is the Louie who got drafted into the Vietnam War. The Louie who cried so hard at our Grandmother's funeral that he fell to his knees by her grave. The Louie who married, fathered two children, divorced, and already had a major heart attack all by age 40. That Louie says...

"Promise me we'll get the family back together."

And I say..., "I promise."

7.

That night...
Again, I feel the presence in my room. But this time it's even stronger. It sends an electrical surge charging through my body that forces me into an upright position.
But my Grandmother is not on my dresser, this time she's standing right next to the bed, over me, her hands raised to the heavens, screaming, "AAAAHHH!!!!"

8.

The following day, I get a letter in the mail.
It reads:

Dear Mr. DaGato:
...our new book, "THE WORLD BOOK OF DAGATOS" is about to be published and it includes individual DaGatos who immigrated to the New World between the 16th and early 20th centuries... You'll even find exciting details about how you can take a family heritage tour back to the DaGato homeland and learn even more about your family's origin.

All for $24.99.
The letter is signed "Louis A. DaGato."

I send away.

9.

That night, I dream again...
I'm standing outside my Grandmother's house, but...it's not as I remember. The house is engulfed by darkness, but the sky behind it is a brilliant white.

I walk down the path toward the house, questioning my every step, my every move. As I reach the porch, I find the front door half open...

I enter.

My Grandmother sits completely motionless on a wooden chair. Then, slowly, she raises her hand, and points toward a long stairway.

When I reach the top, I find the cemetery where my Grandparents are buried, but...there is no plot for my Grandmother and Grandfather's grave. It's gone... I walk up and down the rows, up and down. My eyes scan the names on the tombstones. DaGato. DaGato. I start to weave in and out of the graves. Faster. Reading the names. Faster...

Where is it?

I spot a tombstone made of black marble. A statue of the Virgin Mary on top.

Across the front of the stone, it reads: VALLATA.

10.

Now, the next morning, on my way to work, I find myself...drawn to the store front of a Times Square fortuneteller - Miss Sylvana.

I tell her all about my Grandmother, about the dreams and visions.

I ask, "What do they mean?"

Miss Sylvana explains, "Your Grandmother visits you in your dreams, because you are thinking about your ancestors. She comes to you, because she is a protector. She will watch over you. Tomas... Your relatives call to you. You must go to them. Go to your ancestors."

I say, "Miss Sylvana... They're dead."

She repeats, "Go to your ancestors!"

11.

Wednesday.

    Louie and I meet for lunch.
    I tell him what's been happening, show him the letter.
    He says, "What's this? I didn't write this! It's junk mail!"
    "Louie," I say. "It's a sign."
    He says, "What are you *stunod*?"
    I say, "Not everything in this world can be explained, Lou. But these messages...I think...they're telling me to go to Vallata."
    And then this New York Secretary-type, mid-30's, sitting right next to us, says, "Excuse me..."
    I say, "What?"
    "Oh...," she says. "I'm sorry. I don't mean to pry or anythin', it's just that I overheard youse talkin', and...my people are from the same village that your people are from."
    "Vallata...?" I say.
    "Yeah," she says. "I was there about 10 years ago. Do you still have relatives there?"
    I say, "I don't know."
    She says, "Well, if you do decide to go there...and ya can't find your relatives, ya might wanna look up a man named John Nava. He runs the village hotel. But you should know that it's not really a hotel. It's his house. If ya stay there, ya sleep in his bed, and he goes to sleep somewhere else."
    Then she laughs, slides out of her booth, and starts for the door.
    I say, "Hey, wait! What's your name?"
    She says..., "Sylvana."
    I look at Louie, he looks at me, and from that moment on, all I can think about is my cousin Gerardo, who was the last link to Vallata, my Grandfather's village. I start thinking that maybe I should go to Italy, track him down, visit.

And why not?

Maybe that's what my Grandmother wanted?

Maybe that was the first step to getting the family back together?

I go straight into my Boss's office, and ask if I can take a vacation.

He says, "When?"

I say..., "Next week?"

He says, "You're not going on vacation next week. That brochure still needs massive work. Don't be stupid. Get back to your desk."

I then do the most impulsive thing I have ever done in my adult life - I quit.

I go on-line, and book a flight to Rome, leaving Sunday morning.

12.

Immediately I drive down to Uncle Rudy's to get directions. He lives in my Grandmother and Grandfather's old house. In their retirement years, my Grandparents had moved from Hudson County to the Jersey Shore. It's a trip I'd made with my family hundreds of times, practically every Sunday for years. It's a ride I haven't taken since I was a kid.

The Rascals' "Groovin'" plays.

Back then, our journey would start with my Father driving, my Mother alongside him, my Sister and me in the backseat. We'd cruise down the highway, glancing out the window, not saying much, listening to the radio, 101.1 - WCBS - FM. Cousin Brucie! My Father's favorite.

My Sister would be looking out at the road, her face close to the window, and I'd reach over and...BANG...smack the back of her head so her nose would bounce off the glass.

"Mommy, Thomas hit me!"

My Father would whirl around, start swinging at me.

"Get over here! If I have to pull over...!"

I'd scream, "She started it!"

He'd say, "I don't care! If it happens again we're goin' home!"

Then my Sister and I would both scream, "NO!!!!"

Ten minutes later, it would be my Sister's turn.

She'd start chanting, "Burger Chef...Burger Chef...Burger Chef...Burger Chef..."

While my Father would reply, "No Burger Chef...no Burger Chef..."

My Sister would say, "Burger Chef..."

My Father would say, "No Burger Chef..."

"Burger Chef..."

"No Burger Chef..."

Until, finally, my Sister would scream, "But Dad! I love it! Please stop!"

My Father would say, "You gotta be kidding! You're Grandmother is making homemade ravioli, meatballs, sausage and peppers, veal parmigiano, and you want hamburgers! No! Absolutely not! No Burger Chef!"

My Sister would say, "Yes!"

My Father would say, "No!"

"Yes!"

"No!"

"Yes!"

"NO!!"

Ten minutes after that, my Sister would be distracted, eating a hamburger, plain, nothing on it, not noticing, until...

"Mom! Thomas's on my side of the car!"

My Father would pull off the road, hit the brakes, scream, "That's it! That's it! Thomas you're up front!"

I'd open my door. He open his door like he was coming after me, and I'd run around the back of the car as fast as I could, and jump in the front seat, while my Mother would stomp around the front of the car, and get into the back.

The funny thing is, as scared as I got by my Father's threats, I knew deep down that turning around was out of the question. My Father would *never* miss a Sunday at Grandma's. To him, it meant everything. In fact, the closer we got to the house, the more relaxed he became. He'd start pointing out the sights.
"There's the hospital where your Grandmother use to work."
"There's the church where your cousin Louie got married."
"And there's the firehouse where they had the reception, and you and Joanie won that twist contest!"
"The Twist..."
To this day, whenever my cousin Joanie and I are in the same room together, someone from the family still manages to say, "Remember when you won that twist contest?" And if they have the record, they'll put it on, and try to make us dance.

13.

I pull into my Uncle Rudy's driveway, enter his house without knocking.

He's sitting at the head of the kitchen table, where I'm sure he's been sitting all afternoon. I tell him about my plans to go to Italy, to visit Gerardo. I ask about Vallata, how to get there.

He then proceeds to tell me the story about the Italian immigrant who had come to America, because he heard the streets were paved with gold. When he got here, he found out three things: first, the streets weren't paved with gold; second, they weren't paved at all; and third, he was expected to pave them!

Then Uncle Rudy tells me not how to get to Vallata, but how my Grandfather had come to *Lamerica*.

"You know, your Grandfather rode a mule from Vallata, into the city, and sold it for a one-way ticket to New York. A thousand immigrants on a steam ship. Three weeks it took to Ellis Island. He made it to Jersey City, where he was taken in by the Candelino's, family friends, also from Vallata. If you had no relatives here, you looked up neighbors from your village, and participated in a ritual, a ceremony. The immigrant would clip the nails of their neighbor's youngest child, then place money into the child's hand, making the immigrant an official member of the family. *Adesso fai parte della famiglia.* How close a member, of course, depended on how much money the immigrant gave.

So after being here for a few months, your Grandfather gets approached by a Matchmaker.
'How would you like to get married?'
The Matchmaker then showed your Grandfather a picture of a woman. 'How would you like to marry her? She's from Italy.'
Your Grandfather said, 'Yes...yes... I would like that.'
Now the joke was, the Matchmaker only owned one picture. The picture that he showed your Grandfather is the same one that he showed all the men, and he said the same thing too, 'How would you like to marry her?' Then he would just send to Italy for whose ever available.
Your Grandmother arrived in America, and met your Grandfather for the first time on the docks of Hoboken, and the two of them got married on the spot. And they were married for 55 years."

"Fifty-five years... How do I get to Vallata?"
Uncle Rudy says, "I dunno. I've never been there. I think it's up by Venice."

14.

After checking the web, an atlas, and five travel books, I find out that Vallata is not listed by Venice, in fact, it's not listed anywhere.
I realize there's only one way to find out.
I have to contact my cousin Eugene.

Eugene is my oldest cousin, the first child of the second generation. He was 13 when I was born, and as I grew up, I remembered him as a star athlete, someone who could bench press 300 pounds. I'm intimidated by him...always was. Later, he became a "phys ed" teacher, and with his wife and kids, had traveled and worked all over the world. He'd been to Vallata, and when he returned from Italy, I remember he brought back Pope bottle openers for all the uncles. But during the family split, he'd sided with my Aunt Florence, his mother, and I'd only seen him once in the last ten years...at my Father's funeral.
But he'd been to Vallata. And if anyone knew how to get there, it would be him.

15.

So the next night, I drive over to my Aunt Florence's house, Eugene's mother. She's a widow. Well into her 70s. I haven't seen her in 18 years.
I knock on the front door.
A voice comes from another part of the house, "Who is it?"
I peer off the porch, down the stairs, which run along the side of the house. My Aunt Florence leans out the back door.
"Yeah? What is it?" she says.
Just to make sure, I ask her name. She tells me. Then she says, "Who wants to know? Who are you?"
I say, "I'm Thomas DaGato. Your nephew."

For a second - nothing. She just looks at me. Then...she starts...

"Oh...oh...oh...oh, my God...oh, my God...oh... Look at me...look at me...I got goose bumps...look...look... I was just sitting on the porch an hour ago, and I started thinking about your Father. One hour ago! I was sitting on this porch thinking about your Father and I thought, `What's happened to all the little cousins? What happened to the family?'"

Then, she runs up the stairs, takes my face in her hands, kisses me.

"You see...," she says. "You wake up in the morning, and you never know what God is gonna send ya. Come in the house. You'll eat."

16.

She feeds me...
We talk.
I say, "Can I ask you something?"
She says, "If it has to do with the past - no. I only want to talk about the future."
I say, "Well...it's kind of about the past... I'm going to Italy. I'd like to go to Vallata. But I need to know how to get there."
"Vallata...?" she says.
I say, "Yeah, and I know that Eugene's been there, but I don't know how to get in touch with him."
She says, "I'll have Eugene call you."

17.

Saturday.

I meet Eugene at the batting cages.
The first thing I say is, "Listen...Gene...whatever happened between the family had nothing to do with me. I was a kid."

He says, "I know that."

Then I tell him that I'm going to Italy, that I'd like to visit Gerardo, find Vallata.

He says, "You don't wanna go there. There's nothin' there. Vallata's a little village in Italy. They don't even have runnin' water. You're not gonna find anythin'...touristy. You might not even find Gerardo. I haven't been in touch with him in...16 years, and from what I read, there was a big earthquake over there... I'll give you the address I have, but..."

I say, "Fine. I'm still going. How do I get there?"

He says, "It's about two hours south of Naples."

"Okay..." I say. "Then what?"

"Then ask."

"Then ask?"

He says, "Yeah. It's two hours south of Naples. Then ask."

I say, "What's that suppose to mean?"

"It means," says Eugene. "That I don't remember. You're just gonna have to ask when you get there."

"You don't remember?"

He says, "No. I don't. You just have to know."

I say, "How am I suppose to know?"

He says, "It's in the province of Avellino. I do know that. That's the closest big city. Just get to Avellino. Then ask..."

I say, "I don't speak Italian."

He says, "Then you might have a problem."

18.

I call my Mother and ask her for pictures of the family to take on my trip. She tells me to come by the house. She'll have them ready for me. She doesn't want to go through them while I'm there. For as long as I can remember, she's always kept them locked away.

My Mother sits at the kitchen table, and broods over a photograph.

"Here's one of your Aunt Florence and your cousin Gerardo," she says.

She hands me a picture.

"This one was taken at your Grandmother and Grandfather's 50th wedding anniversary," she says.

She places a photograph down on the table. It's a group shot.

"And here's one of your favorites," she says.

My Mother passes me an old, tattered black and white shot of my Grandmother, my Grandfather, my Sister, and me. I'm holding a James Bond camera gun, and my Sister clutches a stuffed bunny rabbit under her arm.

I say, "Ma...? Is that it? Three pictures?"

She says, "Whatdya wanna bring a whole album?"

I say, "Yeah. Why not?"

"No," she says. "I put `em away. I'm not goin' through `em again."

I say, "I'll go through them. I don't mind. Where are they? In your closet?"

And I start for her room.

But she cuts me off, "NO! No... Those pictures are off-limits. I put `em away. That's it. Now you take what I gave you and be happy. Please... Okay?"

Then she walks away, into the living room.

"Okay..."

I look in on my Mother. She sits alone on the love seat, staring off.

"Lemme ask you...," she says. "Why are you suddenly going to Italy? It's crazy. Why do you want to know so much about the family?"

I say..., "I don't know."

"I think we should have a talk when you get back," she says. "Your Sister. You. Me."

"About what?"

"I'm sorry," she says. "Never mind. I shouldn't have mentioned it. We'll...we'll...talk when you get home."

Then she stands, walks into her bedroom, and closes the door.

"Ma!"

Slow Fade To Black

ACT TWO

The Search For Vallata

19.

Roma!

It's been said, "The beauty of Rome lies in its ruins."
And so I lose myself in the the streets and alleyways of the Ancient City, drinking in 2,000 years of history.

I stare at Michelangelo's *Creation of Adam* on the ceiling of the Sistine Chapel, and it moves me to tears. Water pours out of my right eye, but only my right eye. It's this weird thing I have...

At Trevi Fountain, I make a wish, "I hope I can find Gerardo..."; then I execute a perfect "over-the-left-shoulder coin toss" that...I swear...plops into the water right at the spot where Anita Ekberg stood in LA DOLCE VITA.

Outside the Vatican, I spot a vendor's sign that reads: BUY NOW, PRAY LATER. And on a small table are rosary beads, prayer books...and Pope bottle openers.

20.

The next morning I'm at the train station by 6 a.m. I ask the Guy Behind The Counter for a ticket to Vallata.
He says that he's never heard of it.
I say, "Have you heard of Avellino?"
"*Si*," he says. "Take the 7 a.m. train to Benevento, and switch there for the train to Avellino."

It's two hours from Rome to Naples. Vallata is, "Two hours south of Naples. Then ask." So I figure I have a five hour journey in front of me.

21.

I get on the train. I sit third class. There's six people to a compartment. It's hot. There's no air conditioning. No tinted windows. The seats are bench-style, uncomfortable.

A Conductor comes by to check tickets. I hand him mine. He says, "*Americano?*"

I say, "Yes."

Then he asks to see my passport. I hand that over, and...he starts to put it into his pocket.

I say, "What are you doing?"

He says, "I hold your passport."

And right away I remember reading in my LET'S GO: ITALY tourist guide that, "Your passport is a public document that belongs to your government and may not be withheld without your consent."

So I say, "You don't have to hold my passport."

But he says, "Nonono... *Regolamentos*."

Then I remember Eugene or...somebody saying that, "A passport on the black market can bring thousands of dollars."

I say, "Give me my passport."

He says, "Nono... I hold for you."

I say, "Give me my passport."

But he doesn't answer, doesn't say a word.

I say, "Give me back my passport!"

And then slowly, he hands me back my passport, mumbles *fongule,* and walks away.

22.

The train stops in Benevento. I get off. It's not even a train station. It's a platform in the middle of......Italy. One other person gets off the train with me. A Woman.

I ask, "*Per favore*, *Avellino*?"

She says, "*Si...si...*" She points to the platform.

And we wait...and we wait...and we wait... And then, finally, I see this train coming down the tracks. It's...two cars.

It hisses to a stop. I board, find a seat, and then...we're off, rumbling across the Italian countryside. I look out the window. It's all flatlands and farms. And we're making stops at people's houses, in their front yards, right at the side of the road.

23.

The train stops in Avellino. Avellino, Eugene said, was the closest big city.

Avellino, is five buildings, and road as far as the eye can see in either direction.

I wander into a small store. Behind the counter is an Old Woman in a tattered blue house dress.

I ask, "*Per favore, Vallata.*"

The Old Woman's face lights up. She starts speaking to me in rapid-fire Italian. She talks to me for five minutes. I have no idea what she's saying. Then she places two tickets down on the counter. I assume that I have to take two buses, that I have to switch somewhere.

24.

I go outside. I look for the bus, except...
Where do I stand?

There's a bus stop on that side of the street, and there's a bus stop on this side of the street. No signs. What do I do? It could be either stop. I don't know.

So...

I cross over.

Arbitrary. Totally arbitrary.

I look down the road. An old school bus creaks toward me. It stops. The door's open...

I get on.

I ask the Bus Driver, "*Scusa... Vallata?*"

"*Si...,*" he says. He points to the back of the bus.

I give him one ticket, keep the other, and...

I look at the faces of the people on this bus, and it's the first time that I truly feel that I'm in Italy. These people... Farmers. Construction workers. Carpenters. A mother and her daughter. They sit in stone silence, but their eyes follow me as I proceed down the center aisle towards the back of the bus.

We travel through a series of small towns, then turn onto a highway. I look out the window. There's nothing in front of us but road, and a mountain off in the distance. But one hour later, the mountain is no longer in the distance. It's all around us. We're at the base. The bus stops in this tiny village, and it must be the end of the line too, because everyone is filing off. I grab my bag and follow.

On the street, I ask the Bus Driver, "*Scusa... Dove Vallata?*"

He nods with his head at the bus in front of ours.

"*Vallata,*" he says. "*Vallata...*"

25.

I run over to Bus #2. It's half-filled. The Driver never even asks for my ticket. I take a seat in the back, look at my watch. It's noon. I've been on the road for five hours. "I'm a dead man. They'll never find my body. No one will ever find my body."

The bus pulls away from the curb, and slowly begins to wind its way up the mountain. Circling. Circling. Circling. And there is only one lane. So when we get to a blind spot in a turn, the bus comes to a complete stop, the driver hits the horn, sees if anyone is coming the other way; then proceeds. The law of the road is the bigger vehicle rules.

Up we go.

Higher and higher and higher and higher...

The transmission, I think, starts making this grinding sound that comes up through the bottoms of my feet, and doesn't stop until my eardrums are vibrating, and the fillings in my teeth start to shake loose. And I can feel the altitude changing. My jaw cracks. My ears pop. I'm starting to feel lightheaded. I'm having trouble breathing. And it's hot. IT IS HOT. I'm sweating right through my shirt. I need air, oxygen. I try to open the window, but I can't. It's stuck. I look down. There are no guardrails. There is two feet of room between the bus, and the edge of a cliff. I start thinking, "What if the driver is really hungover?" Then, halfway down the mountain, I can see a Fiat wrapped around a tree. I think, "They didn't even bother to tow it! They left it there as a reminder!"

"Two hours south of Naples. Then ask." I mean what could I have been thinking? I quit my job! Where am I going? There are no signs! Nothing! Nothing! Gerardo? My relatives? I don't even know if they're alive!

I lean into The Guy In Front Of Me, and say, "I might get sick... I just want you to know."

I drop my head down on the seat in front of me...

And then I feel a tap on my arm. It's the Woman Across The Aisle. She's about my age, has sympathetic eyes. She offers me a sip from her bottled water.

"*Grazie.*"

"You're welcome," she says.

"You speak English?"

She says, "*Un' po.*"

I say, "I'm looking for a place called Vallata..."

She says, "I know Vallata."

I say, "Where is it?"

She says, "Before my village. My village last stop."

"Vallata is the second to last stop?"

"*Si,*" she says.

I say, "I'm trying to find my cousin." Then I show her my pictures, my addresses. I point to Gerardo. "Do you know him?"

"No," she says. "But I can find address. I take you. Then I walk to my village."

I say, "*Grazie.*"

"*Prego,*" she says, and she laughs.

"What's your name?" I ask.

"Sylvana," she says.

"Sylvana..."

26.

The bus stops in a little square. Sylvana and I exit. The first thing I do is look at my surroundings. There's a monument. An island with three Mobil gas pumps. A half-dozen cars. That's all. Sylvana stands a few feet away talking to Two Young Men. She shows them my pictures and addresses. Then she turns and tells me that the Two Young Men know the address...and they'll take us.

27.

We climb into their car. The second the engine turns over, the radio kicks in - Creedance Clearwater Revival. And it's LOUD. *Fortissimo!*

"I Heard It Through The Grapevine" plays.

I say to Sylvana, "Are these guys cab drivers?"
She says, "No."
I say, "You know, this would never happen in New York. You would never give your bags to two strangers outside the Port Authority, and say, `Could you help me find my relatives?'"
And she says, "Tomas, sometimes you have to trust."

We drive four or five blocks. There are chickens running across the street. There are women with wash baskets balanced on their heads walking along the side of the road. There's an Elderly Woman, standing on the corner, dressed just like my Grandmother in the dreams, in widow black, her hands raised to the heavens, screaming, "AAAAHHHH!!!!"

Music FADES.

28.

We come to a stop. Sylvana and I climb out of the car. There's a cobblestone sidewalk leading straight up.
We walk to the top.
There, in front of us, is a little brick house. There's no front door, either. There are plastic beads strung in its place. Sylvana walks right inside, doesn't knock, doesn't wait for someone to come out and answer the beads. She just marches right in the house.
I put my bag on the ground, and...peek in the doorway.

Sylvana stands in the kitchen and talks to an Older Woman. She's about 60. Behind her is Another Woman, who appears to be in her mid-30s, and a Young Boy. The matriarch stands with her arms folded across her chest. She seems annoyed, and judging from the enormous pot of sauce boiling on the stove, it's because we've interrupted her cooking.

"Sylvana," I say. "Please tell her that I am Thomas DaGato. I am a cousin from America. I've come to the village to find my family."

Sylvana translates. As she does, I approach the matriarch, hand her my pictures. She takes them, examines each one carefully; then begins to laugh. The others huddle around her. She and Sylvana exchange words.

Sylvana turns to me, and says, "Her name is Michelina. Mother to Gerardo. This is wife to Gerardo. This is son to Gerardo. They visit from *Firenze* - Florence. Gerardo will come tonight."

Then an Older Man comes through the front door. Michelina excitedly tells him who I am. His name is Rocco. He is Gerardo's father. He's been working in the fields.

Rocco then tells Sylvana to tell me that they would like me to stay for lunch.

I say, "*Grazie.*"

Together they say, "*Prego!*" And we laugh. Then Michelina pushes past us, goes outside. She picks up my bag, and takes it back into the house. "*Arrivederci!*" she says. She waves her hand at Sylvana, ushers her out of the house, until she's gone...never to be seen again.

"*Arrivederci...*"

29.

Two hours later lunch is *almost* over. I'm having a cannoli, an espresso, and a brandy.

Michelina is in the kitchen. I can hear her rummaging around. I silently pray that she doesn't bring in anything more to eat or drink.

She doesn't.

Instead, she brings in a cigar box, which she places in front of me.

Except...

The box is filled with pictures.

"Gerardo," she says. "America."

And I realize that these are the pictures that Gerardo took when he was visiting. I begin sorting through them, and... I find a black and white picture of my Grandmother, my Grandfather, my Sister, and me. I'm holding a James Bond camera gun, and my Sister clutches a stuffed bunny rabbit under her arm.

Michelina puts her hand on my shoulder, says, "*Dormi a casa mia.*" I search for the words in my Italian/English dictionary. They mean, "You sleep in my house."

Rocco dumps the box of pictures onto the table, points to members of the family. I do my best to tell him each person's history. Alive. Dead. Married. Divorced. When I finish, Rocco takes pen and paper, and sketchs the family tree back three generations, starting with my Great Grandfather, my Grandfather, his brothers and sisters. Rocco tells me that we are sitting in the house that my Grandfather was born in. Then he points down at a name - Graziano. "*Vive*," he says. Meaning that he is alive, and he gestures to say that he is living here in Vallata.

I grab Rocco's hand. "Take me to him..."

30.

We walk to the center of town. Michelina has me by one arm, Gerardo's Wife has me by the other. Rocco walks behind us with Gerardo's Son. We walk like a proud parade. I feel like Gulliver. I tower over them. They're all my Father's size... People poke their heads out open windows to watch us go by. Others, friends of the family, join in the march, asking all about me as me move on. Five minutes later, as we approach another house, our procession has grown to more than a dozen people.

31.

We stop 20 yards away. Outside, is an old, old man sitting on a wooden chair. Even though it's the end of summer, he's wearing a wool sport jacket and vest. He has on a cap. He leans on a cane.

Rocco approaches the man, says something in Italian; then calls me over. As I move toward them...it becomes obvious. The resemblance unmistakeable. He is my Grandfather's brother. His name is Graziano, Rocco says. He is 88 years old.

There's a silent pause as the parade forms a semi-circle around us. Graziano and I shake hands. I show him my pictures. He looks down at the one of my Grandmother, my Grandfather, my Sister, and me... Then his hands begin to tremble. He kisses the picture. Then he begins to cry, and he leans his head into my hip. I stroke his hair. He struggles to his feet, wraps his arms around my neck, and kisses my cheek.

32.

After a few moments, we go inside. Graziano is still crying, but he can't stop talking about my Grandfather.

"*Mio fratello*," he says.

He tells me how Grandpa had sent him money from America every month so that he could build his house. The house we were standing in...

We sit down in the kitchen. Graziano places a jug of wine down on the table, pours me a glass. I drink and... I drift back in time. It's Sunday afternoon. I'm drinking wine from a shot glass that my Grandfather has poured for me at the dinner table. It's the same wine... The exact recipe. Even the smell is the same.

33.

We stay at Graziano's for more than an hour...drinking wine. By the time we get back to Rocco and Michelina's, I'm in need of a nap.

I lie down in the bedroom, and...

I'm 11 years old. We're at my Aunt Florence's house. Everyone is at the kitchen table, yelling back and forth, standing, red faced, spitting, crying, flailing their hands, cursing, pointing fingers, until finally my Father is banging his fists down on the kitchen table, screaming, *"Stai-zito! Stai-zito!"*

I wake up.

I stay there at the end of the bed, for what seems like a long, long time.

34.

"Tomas! Tomas!"

It's later that night. Gerardo is saying my name over and over again. We're at the dinner table. There's a party in my honor.

"My cousin...!" Gerardo says. "I can't believe my eyes! You're here!"

In the two hours since his arrival from their home in Florence, Gerardo has sat by my side. He teaches high school English now, and talks at length about his trip to America, which is interesting, because his stories about America are nothing at all like the stories he had left behind.

When Gerardo first arrived in the U.S., he gave rocks to all the relatives with VALLATA hand painted on each stone. That we both remember... But while the rest of Gerardo's memories are filled with images of the Statue of Liberty and Ellis Island, my memories are filled with images of Gerardo as a teenage Marcello Mastroianni. I mean even at age 11 I knew that whatever it was he had...I wanted some. His prowess was so reknowned, that on a visit to Niagara Falls, he managed to run into an old girlfriend...from Vallata. And even though he could barely speak English, that didn't stop him from going over to the best looking bridesmaid at my cousin's wedding, and saying, "Would you screw me?"

And she looked right in his face, and said, "I'm in room 314..."

I remember going with him and my Father to the docks in New York to see him off, back to Italy. We stood on the ship with him, and when the whistle blew, telling us that it was time to go, time for us to go back to land, he started to cry, and he grabbed my Father and wouldn't let go. On the deck, Gerardo held onto a ball of yarn, while my Father held the other end and stood on land. Now this was a custom that dated back to the early immigrants. The point being that the ball would unwind, and the wind would keep the yarn in the air long after those on the ship and those on the dock had vanished from view. But before the ship had even left port, Gerardo had dropped the yarn, and was already holding hands with the woman standing next to him!

He was...a family legend.

"Tell me!" Gerardo shouts. "Tell me everything!"

And he barrages me with questions about my life, about the U.S.A.

When I tell him about the problems back home with Uncle Rudy and Aunt Florence, he just...shakes his head, looks off in the distance.

And then Gerardo is on his feet, waving his hands around the room. "A toast," he says. "To my cousin... God bless the family!"

Then Gerardo runs over to a portable record player in the corner.

I say, "Play me something Italian!"

He says, "I know what you like!"

And I watch as an old 45 drops down on the turntable.

"The Twist" plays. A brief dance. Music FADES.

35.

On the morning that I leave, all the relatives come down to the square to send me off. They bring me prosciutto sandwiches for my trip back down. They cry. They wave their handkerchiefs. And I can't help but think of my Grandfather, who had made this same journey more than 80 years before, on the back of a mule...

As the bus arrives, Gerardo steps forward, says, "Goodbye, Tomas. Goodbye."

I say, "Gerardo... Come back to America. Come visit."

But he says, "No... I don't think so, Tomas. I have a family now. There are many bills. No... I'm sorry..."

And in that moment I realize that I may never see Gerardo again...

Then, suddenly, Graziano makes his way through the crowd. He hands me two bottles of wine, says something in Italian.

Gerardo listens, translates, says, "I told Graziano about America. The problems...your aunt...your uncle. He says you should take this wine and drink it with your family. He says your Grandfather would be very happy."

I shake hands with Graziano, board the bus, and as the doors close behind me, Gerardo yells, "I'll send my son to visit you."

Slow Fade To Black

ACT THREE

Adesso Fai Parte Della Famiglia

36.

J.F.K. International Airport

I step off the plane, and the first thing I see is someone holding a sign over their face that reads: DAGATO.
It's Louie!
He gives me a ride back to my Mother's house, where all the relatives are waiting, and I tell everyone...my Italy story. But before I can even finish, Uncle Rudy grabs the wine out of my hands.
"I can't take it!" he screams. "Gimme the wine! I gotta try it!"
He pulls the cork, pours a glass.
"It's Grandpa's wine...," he says. "It's Grandpa's wine..."

Later, Louie corners me outside.
He says, "What are you doin' with the other bottle?"
I say, "I'm bringing it to Aunt Flo's. I'm giving it to Eugene."
"I havta go with you," Louie says. "This is it. This is our chance to get the family back together. We'll ask everyone."
"What about Uncle Rudy," I say. "He's not gonna go."
"He will if you ask him," Louie says.
"Me?"

"Yeah, you!" Louie says. "You just went back to Grandpa's village! Didn't you see Uncle Rudy's face when you were tellin' that story? The last time he was quiet that long he was asleep. Believe me. There has never been a better chance. He'll go."

I say, "C'mon, Lou..."

"Tommy," he says. "You promised me. You promised to help me get the family back together. Now I'm askin' you to make good on that promise. Please..."

37.

Two days later, I drive down to Uncle Rudy's.

"Why don't you come with us?" I say. "We can get this over with once and for all. Everyone can apologize... We can get all the relatives together one more time? Wouldn't that be something? I mean if I hadn't contacted cousin Eugene the entire connection to Vallata, to Grandpa's village, would've been lost forever. Our history! C'mon, Uncle Rudy. Come with us. What do you say? Huh?"

"How could you go visit someone whose turned their back on the rest of the family? No...no... I'm not goin'. No. You go. You wanna go, you go. But I want nothin' ta do with 'em. I go there, we're gonna fight. And I'm too old for fightin'."

I say, "There's not going to be..."

He says, "No! I'm not goin'. And I don't wanna hear another word about it. Okay? Not from you, not from anyone."

In the end, it's down to just Louie and me, visiting Eugene and my Aunt Flo.

38.

On the big day, we're in Louie's car, talking.

He says, "It was a nice thought, I suppose, tryin' to get everyone together, but...looks like it's never gonna happen. Once Grandma and Grandpa died, that was that. End of family. No more Sundays. No more Sundays... There was nowhwere to go. There was nothin' left to hold us together. And what was left... We fought over 'til nobody's speaking to nobody... Tommy, I'll always be your cousin, but things have changed. We just have to accept that. Your Mother's a grandmother now. You're an uncle. Your Sister's a mother. You have a nephew. That's your family. Don't screw it up."

39.

We arrive at Aunt Flo's.

Louie and Eugene stand on opposite sides of the screen door. I hang back, watch...as 18 years of separation...slips away.

Eugene comes outside, extends his hand toward Louie, says, "Hey... Good to see you."

Louie, grabs Eugene in a bear hug, and pounds him on the back.

When we sit down to eat, Louie squeezes my leg under the table as if he can't believe that it's really happening, that we're really there. And Louie talks, talks about everything, his job, his kids, the old days...

But all this talk about the past makes Eugene tense. He crushes a beer cap between his fingers, rips the label off his bottle.

Louie senses this and changes the subject.

"Tommy," he says. "Show Eugene your pictures from Italy."

But Eugene goes through them like they were a deck of cards, pausing only at a shot of Michelina, Rocco, me.

"Would you look at this picture," Eugene says. "Look at you... You're a giant next to these people."

Louie says, "*Stai-zito*, huh..."

Eugene says, "What? I was just saying how Tommy looks like..."

"Shut up!" Louie says. "*Stai-zito*. All right?"

40.

Later that night, that's all I can think about. Louie telling Eugene, "*Stai-zito...*"

But over what...?

And then it begins to make sense.

Everything...

41.

I drive to my Mother's house. She greets me at the door.

I say, "We have to talk."

She says, "What is it?"

"I need to know where I'm from."

She says, "What do you mean?"

"You know what I mean."

She says, "No. I don't."

"Am I adopted?"

My Mother looks at the floor, her hands folded in her lap, she says, "Yes... You are."

My Mother tells this story.

She got pregnant, and...nine months later she went into labor on the exact day that the Doctor predicted. The Baby, a girl, was born with mucus lodged in her throat. The Doctors tried to clear the Baby's throat, but...they couldn't...and...she died.

My Father was devastated. The next day, he returned all the gifts from the baby shower; then went to my Mother's hospital room, climbed into her bed, and the two of them...,"cried like anything."

Afterwards, my Mother would say, "I'm mad at God right now."

And for the next five years...although they tried...my Mother could not get pregnant.

Finally, her Doctor suggested, "If you want a child that badly, why don't you adopt?"

So...

They did.

They went to an adoption agency that was run by a Catholic diocese. Their names were put on a waiting list, and two years later they received a letter stating, "Mr. and Mrs. DaGato... We have a child for you. It's a boy."

It was January. My parents drove uptown and bought baby clothes at Raifee's Youth Center, everything blue. At the adoption agency, my parents stood at the counter, and watched as I was brought down the hall. My Mother said I had the biggest eyes.

My Biological Mother was 18 years old, unmarried. I was taken from her immediately after birth, she never saw me. I was of Irish, Polish, and Italian descent. I was born three months earlier, on October 22.

My Father heard this and started to cry...

He was born on October 22.

Three years later...my Mother gave birth to my Sister.

And then the story cuts...

My Grandmother has just died, and she has left no will, and there's an argument at my aunt's house. My Uncle Rudy accuses my Aunt Florence of going to my Grandmother's house, and stealing things, jewelry... My Aunt Florence accuses my Uncle Rudy of not properly dividing the money and house my Grandmother has left behind.

And then my Father suggests a compromise.

"Why not leave everything to the nieces and nephews?"

Uncle Rudy, he nods in my direction, and says, "C'mon... He's not blood."

And Aunt Florence says, "Yeah. He's not one of us."

My Father bangs his fist down on the kitchen table, and screams, *"Stai-zito! Stai-zito!"* Then, he turns, and says, "Thomas, go outside."

I say, "Why?"

He says, "Go outside! Go play with your cousins!"

I say, "But..."

He says, "GO!!"

And I run out of the house.

That night, my Father said this to my Mother... That I should never know that I was adopted. Ever. That if the other kids from school, or the neighborhood, ever found out, that they might use it against me. That my Sister might use it against me. If he ever finds out, my Father said. He'll turn his back on the family. Then he made my Mother promise that I would never know. He went to everyone of the relatives, and made them promise that I would never know. He locked away all our family pictures... And eight years later, on his deathbed, my Father made my Mother renew her promise, and reluctantly, she agreed.

When my Mother finishes her story, she says, "I see on these t.v. talk shows all the time about adoptees who search for their biological parents... Are you gonna do that?"

42.

I run, I do not walk, straight into therapy.

I get a new job doing public relations at a non-profit organization.

I find a new girlfriend - Sylvia. Close enough...

Then, a few months later, early on a Sunday morning, my Mother calls, and says, "Thomas... Your cousin Louie died."

Louie had gone to a diner around the corner from his house. He sat at the counter, ordered coffee. Then, Jacqueline M. Ryan, the town undertaker, walked through the door. Louie went to high school with her, use to joke with her all the time. As soon as she sat down, Louie said, "Hey, Jackie! How's business?" Then, he turned to the Waitress, and said, "A person could die before he gets a refill around here." And that was the last thing he ever said, "A person could die before he gets a refill around here." His heart seized. His head hit the counter, and... The Waitress came over and thought he was foolin' around. She said, "Louie, knock it off. Come on... It's not funny." Then she realized it was no joke...that...he was dead.

43.

The next day Louie is laid out at the Jacqueline M. Ryan Home For Funerals.

When Aunt Florence and Eugene arrive, the room fills with nervous tension. All eyes turn to my Uncle Rudy.

Would there be a fight?

But no...

Uncle Rudy stays on one side of the room. Aunt Florence stays on the other. No acknowledgements.

On the day of the burial, Eugene and I are the first to volunteer as pallbearers.

I step forward to pay my final respects, and place two shot glasses inside the casket.

"I'll have one, if you have one..."

At the cemetary, there's the sound of car doors slamming, whispers, and muffled cries.

We walk across the graveyard's soil.

We march past the grave of our Grandmother.

We march past the grave of our Grandfather.

We march until we reach the hole in Mother Earth that will take our cousin Louie...my favorite...forever.

And as I stand there, and look at the faces of my relatives, I remember the promise I made to Louie that we would get the family back together. And on instinct I reach down and I grab Uncle Rudy's hand. Then I reach down and grab my Mother's hand, and it causes a chain reaction, that spreads to my Sister, my Brother-In-Law, cousin Joanie, Eugene, Aunt Florence, out and around and thru all the relatives until it comes back full circle to my Uncle Rudy. And for a few seconds...a few seconds...the family is together...

Slow Fade To Black

END OF PLAY

Long Gone Daddy

For Sarah and Olivia

PRODUCTION HISTORY

Long Gone Daddy was first performed by the author in a Salon format that toured homes throughout Hoboken and Jersey City, NJ, from 2015 – 2016. Voices were provided alternately by Andrew Baldwin and Steven Haworth. It was produced by Elizabeth DiCandilo and Zabrina Stoffel for Mile Square Theatre.

The play subsequently opened at Mile Square Theatre in Hoboken, NJ, on July 20, 2016. The production was directed by Chris O'Connor; set and lighting design by Matt Fick; sound design by Michael Blaskewicz; and the production stage manager was Sarah Martins.

THOMAS DAGATO	Joseph Gallo

TIME: The not so distant past…

PLACE: Hoboken, New Jersey
  New York City
  The surrounding suburbs.

CHARACTER: A man in the prime of life – THOMAS DAGATO. He wears a dress shirt and tie (slightly loosened), blue jeans, running shoes.

The actor playing THOMAS should read all boldfaced titles.

VOICES can be pre-recorded, or in the unplugged version, read by the actor playing THOMAS.

ACT ONE

(In the dark, we HEAR the sound of a keyboard, typing - LIGHTS UP.)

That night Bruce Springsteen and the E-Street Band were playing Madison Square Garden.

And so I log-on to Ticketmaster periodically for most of the day, hoping for tickets to drop, and then it's non-stop, full force from 3 – 5 pm – find tickets, find tickets, find tickets until they knock me off the site.

I decide I *have* to see him, and my Wife and I head out to the Garden to scalp.

We do a lap around the arena, and…nada.

Nothing.

We go into The Blarney Rock Pub to re-group.

I make a sign out of a place mate – NEED 2 – and again we hit the street this time to the corner of 32nd and 7th Avenue.

Fifteen minutes later this Guy and his Wife walk up to us…middle age, wearing way too much faded denim, matching white-on-white Nikes from…like…10 years ago.

Real Jersey.

The guy says, "I have two."

I say, "How much?"

He says, "Here. They're free. *Just take 'em…*"

I quickly glance at the tickets so as not to make a scene – Section 428.

They are as far away as you can possibly get!

No wonder he's giving them away!

But…
We're going to see Bruce.
It's one of my favorite sentences in the English language.

It's my Wife's and my tenth show together, and overall my 52nd. When we started dating my Wife had never seen Bruce before, and I took her to her first show at the now shuttered Meadowlands Arena. And so began this ritual of us seeing Bruce *together*, and I *love rituals*, because they give you this illusion that life goes on forever.

We get inside the Garden, and I say, "Let's not even go to those seats. Let's walk straight toward the stage, and see how close we can get…"

And we end up finding two empty seats in Section 73…*and we stay there for the entire show*, which starts promptly at 8:15. House lights still up. No fanfare. And then there they are…on-stage…Bruce Springsteen and the E-Street Band.

(We HEAR the SOUND of a live audience.)

"Is there anyone alive out there?"

And that's all it takes for me.
That one line.
Because I *never* feel more alive than when I'm at a Bruce Springsteen show.

Bruce attacks the microphone, launches straight into "Badlands." The crowd is mega-into-it…singing along…screaming back at the stage, and it…does…not…stop.

Song two, four words.
"Adam Raised A Cain."

By now I am weeping openly.
It does not get any better than "Adam Raised a Cain."
But then he follows it with "She's The One"…and it just did.
And what makes this extra special is that "She's The One" is a song my Wife and I have never heard together live, and it's *our song.* Ever since I first saw her in the backroom of the old Maxwell's with her red hair fallin', and her *green* eyes that shine like the midnight sun, she's been my rock and roll girl. And the two of us we start…*flipping out!*
Bruce pleads out the lyrics, shouts the first chorus up to the heavens, "Ohhhh!!!! She's the one! Yeah!"
And my Wife, she spins around, looks right into my eyes, and says…, "I think we should have a baby!"

(Pause.)

And it's like her words push me back one full step.
I find myself speechless.
I'm suddenly……*aroused.*
My Wife, she throws her arms around my neck, and hugs me harder than ever before.
And that's how we ride out the song.

I stagger off to get us some drinks.
On the way, I hit the men's room where I find myself re-enacting that clichéd movie scene where I'm looking at myself in the bathroom mirror, and I'm wondering…, "Who are you?"
My Wife wants to have a baby.
I mean I knew this day would come eventually, but it's not like I even notice babies. If someone hands me a baby, I hand them right back.

How could *I* be a father?
My biological father abandoned me.
My adoptive father he……uh…
A child's future would be in my hands?

The next day I go running.

I'm doing a circle around Hoboken.
I have my ear buds in, my music is set to shuffle, and THE ORIGINAL DRUM BATTLE comes on.
My Dad's favorite album.
It features a drum challenge between Buddy Rich and Gene Krupa.

(We hear music from "The Original Drum Battle.")

Flashback.

It's the summer before my senior year in high school.
I walk into the house of my adopted parents, and my Mom says, "Your Dad bought you something."
I say, "What?"
She says, "It's a surprise. Go upstairs in the attic."
And I go upstairs, and there's my Dad setting up this beautiful 1964 Ludwig, black pearl, Ringo Starr drum kit in mint condition.
"I bought 'em for $200," he says. *"In a garage sale.* This guy didn't know what he was sittin' on. They're worth 20 times what I paid for 'em. *(Pause.)* I bought 'em for you."
Now my Dad *use to* play the drums…in fact, the first time my Mom laid eyes on him he was behind the kit in this nightclub in Union City.
And so I say, "I don't play the drums."
But my Dad hands me a set of sticks, and he says, "Nah. Sit down. Play."

And I bang around for a couple of minutes...I don't know what I'm doing.

My Dad tries to give me a few pointers, and then he starts to do something that he rarely does.

He starts to *really* talk to me.

Now he's a quiet guy my Dad, I love him, but he doesn't talk much about anything let alone feelings. The only feeling I ever get from him is the one he brings home from work. He's a fireman. And sometimes he takes that feeling right into the bedroom with him and he lies down.

"Shhh...," my Mother says. "Daddy had a rough day. You have to be quiet..."

Fires.

Explosions.

The Jaws of Life.

And so it surprises me when he says, "Thomas...you know...I've been workin' a looong time. Almost 25 years. You work until you retire. And that's when you can start to enjoy life...*when you retire*. And so I...uh...I been savin' up my sick days. I stopped takin' vacation days. I'm stock-pilin' as much time as I can so that I can retire at the end of next year. I even got this calendar in the basement and I'm X'ing off the days. And you know what I wanna do? Once I'm done? I wanna take you, your Mother, your sister to Hawaii. That's somethin' I always wanted to do. Go to Hawaii. And you know what else I wanna do? I wanna get *you* on the fire department before I leave. This way you'll be set for life. You can start your own family."

I hand my Dad back the drums sticks......and I go downstairs.

Let me tell you about how my Dad became a fireman.

He had been playing drums in this jazz band, and one night they showed up for a gig in Atlantic City at the exact same time as *another* band.

Both bands had been booked to play the same club on the same night!

And they flipped a coin to see who would get to play, and......my Dad's band lost… and he came home with no money.

My Mother went..., "This won't do."

Now my Mom's brother, my Uncle Stretch, was already a fireman, and I don't know if my Mother called my uncle, or if my uncle took some personal initiative, but…one day, my Uncle Stretch comes over to the house, gives my Dad a fire department application, and says, "You're coming on."

My Mom placated my Dad by saying, "You know when you retire, you can pick-up the drums again, and then you can play until your heart's content…"

And now my Dad was ready to retire.

Those drums weren't for me.

They were for him.

He wanted me to have *his* life.

(Music from "The Original Drum Battle" returns.)

And then I'm back in Hoboken.

I've run full-circle.

(He shuts off the music, takes the speaker buds out of his ears, and looks up at his building.)

I enter our apartment…
My Wife is in the bedroom.
I see her from behind as I enter the room.
All she's wearing is a black G-string.

And as they say in hockey..., "We pull the goalie."

Two months later, my Wife comes out of the bathroom, and says, "I'm pregnant!"

Then she shows me the little white stick.

And just like that she changes before my eyes.

One day, I watch her as she moves around the apartment...and even though her daily wardrobe now includes something called stretchy pants, I still think...she looks beautiful.

But she also seems more...*fragile*.

Then she makes a call on her cell phone.

It seems to me that she's starting to spend an excessive amount of time on her cell.

Talking.

To her mother.

The only time my Wife *talks* on the phone is when it's an emergency!

It's almost as if she's turning...*inward.*

And it's not like I feel rejected or anything.

But I realize that I'm having a difficult time connecting to her pregnancy.

I visit my friend MJ.

I've known him since the eighth grade.

He lives uptown in the Shipyard Building.

And while I'm someone who always seems to be engaged in some kind of inner dialogue, MJ's the kind of guy who has something to say about virtually everything, whether he agrees with you or not...for instance, he recently told me that he didn't listen to Springsteen anymore.

He didn't like anyone telling him their politics. He just wanted him to play his music, and get off the stage.

He told me, "I'm not saying Springsteen's lost it...*live he's a phenomenal force*...I'm saying he lost me. I listen to different music now."

And this after the two of us had seen Springsteen at: the Stone Pony in Asbury Park, where we were so close to the stage...we could have knocked over his mic stand; in Rome, where a taxi driver famously asked us, "The Boss. What does he mean..., 'Born to Run'?"; and, in Minneapolis, where *Prince* sat in the seat right next to mine, and at one point in the show I high-fived him...and almost knocked him over.

MJ and I have had some times together.

MJ also has twin girls.

He knows a thing or two about a thing or two.

We stand in the middle of his apartment and I cannot believe the amount of upheaval that I see in every corner of the house, clothes on the floor, toys scattered everywhere, dishes and cups on ever surface.

I tell him that my Wife's pregnant...

MJ says, "You must be excited."

He's holding one of the kids, who has snot running uncontrollable out of her nose, while her sister cruises around the apartment with a wooden spoon smacking down on everything that gets in her path.

"The problem is I'm not excited," I say. "I feel...*conflicted*."

"Hm...," he says. "...hold that thought...."

Then he hands me the kid that he's holding then goes after the other kid and rips the wooden spoon out of her hands just as she reaches his flat screen television.

"What are you *conflicted* about?" MJ asks. "Stop. You have no other choice. *The baby is coming.* You're going to take to it right away. It's fun."

And then the kid I'm holding bursts into tears and starts screaming at the top of her lungs.

(We HEAR the SOUND of a baby screaming.)

"How is it fun?"

And then his wife Christina comes in from the other room takes the screaming kid out of my hands, and says, "It's fun because he gets to go to work. I'm the one who has to stay home all day…with the kids."

MJ pulls me into the hallway.

"Look…," he says. "No one is ever *ready* to become a father. *I was petrified.*"

"And?"

"I found out that I was petrified of all the wrong things."

"Like what?"

"I was petrified that I would be completely consumed. That I would lose having any time to myself…I wouldn't be me anymore, etc., etc."

"That *doesn't* happen?"

"No. That does happen. Your life as you know it is *definitely* over. But that's not what you should be petrified of…," he says. "What you should be petrified of is the constant worry, 'Is the baby all right?' Because that's the job. *To take care of the baby.* You need to put your focus…"

"…on being a father."
"No."
"No?"
"On being a Dad," he says. "You become a father as soon as the baby is born. Anyone can become a father. *But that doesn't make you a Dad.* Being a Dad is something that you earn."

"And when will I earn the right to be called Dad?"

He says…, "The universe will tell you."

Blackout

ACT TWO

(LIGHTS rise on THOMAS, seated in a doctor's office.)

The next day I go with my Wife to see her OBGYN.

    I decide to put my focus on understanding what my Wife is going through.
    I want to connect!
    And the first step is to make sure that she and the baby are okay.
    As we sit in the waiting room I start flipping through Pregnancy Magazine, pages and pages and pages, essentially saying the same thing over and over…, "This is going to be *really* hard."

    VOICE 1: In the baby's first year…you will spend a minimum of $10,000 additional dollars.
    VOICE 2: In the baby's first year…you will lose between 300 and 400 hours of sleep.
    VOICE 3: In the baby's first year…you will change their diaper on average 2,000 times.

    I turn to my Wife, and say, "Are you *sure* that you want to do this?"

    And then the office door opens.

    (We HEAR entrance MUSIC, over the top, very dramatic.)

    Filling the frame is the O-B-G-Y-N.

He has this tidal wave of thick white hair.

His hands are behind his back, he *inspects* the waiting room.

He's wearing a crisp, military blue dress shirt and over it…a starched white lab coat…he looks very…*Gestapo-esque*.

My Wife and I both stand to greet him, she says, "This is my husband Thomas."

The O-B-G-Y-N says…, "Present and accounted for."

Then he gestures for her to enter the examining room.

I trail behind, but the O-B-G-Y-N stops me with a hand.

He follows my Wife inside, and…closes the door.

That night…

…as we lie in bed, my Wife asks, "Are you going to be here for me?"

"What?" I say.

"Are you going to be here for me?"

"Of course I'm going to be here for you. I love you…"

"Are you committed to being the father of this child?"

(Pause.)

"Yes."

And then we talk…about the future.

She'll go back to work after three months. We both work in education so two paychecks…definitely a must. The baby will go into daycare full-time. We'll split the housework as always 50/50.

And so with everything seemingly settled, we drift off to sleep…at least she does, anyway. I still have her words in my head…, "*Are you going to be here for me?*"

We hit the three month mark.

I start announcing, "My Wife's pregnant!"
And while it does make fatherhood seem a bit more real, I find I'm not prepared for the *attitude* I get from other fathers.

VOICE 1: Your Wife's pregnant?
"Yeah."
VOICE 1: Tell her I'm happy for her.
"I will."
VOICE 1: I hope *you're* in shape.
"What?"

VOICE 2: You're Wife's pregnant?
"Yeah."
VOICE 2: Congratulations!"
"Thank you."
VOICE 2: *Get ready.*
"For what?"
VOICE 2: You'll see.
"What does that mean?"

VOICE 1: Your life is about to change.
VOICE 2: Your life isn't your own anymore.
VOICE 1: Your life is sooo over.
VOICES 1 & 2: It's the land of no return!!!!

I agree to take a Childbirth Class.

My Wife arrives late to the first session.
"My ankles are swollen," she says. "I got here as fast as I could."

We're handed a black doll, a practice baby.

I grab the baby by the arm, and as I turn…it slips out of my hand, and falls to the floor.

Everyone stops to look.

The Teacher continues, "Now picture the baby seeing you for the first time."

I pick the doll up off the floor, and say, "This baby's going to think…, 'You ain't my daddy.'"

No one laughs.

My Wife takes the doll out of my hands.

"Would you knock it off!" she says. "You're going to be a father. Act like one."

A few nights later, I sit down to pay our bills.

And suddenly……I feel like I can't breathe.
I feel *completely overwhelmed.*
I'm having chest pains.
It's like I'm dying.

I go to see our Doctor who tells me that my symptoms point to common anxiety. There's even a phrase for it…

I tell my Wife.

"I'm psychologically pregnant!"

Silence.

It's the kind of silence that says, "You didn't really just say that did you?"

And it's followed by laughter.

Non-stop laughter.

"Please," my Wife says. "You don't really count right now."

I don't really count?

There's a baby shower for my Wife in New York.

When I arrive at the party's conclusion, I am overwhelmed at the amount of *plastic* my Wife has received. We take a cab back to Hoboken, and on my lap I hold something called a co-sleeper. On the front of the box in bold-faced print it reads:

VOICES 1, 2, 3: Warning! Failure to follow instructions could result in serious injury or death!

I point this out to my Wife, "Does that mean *I'm* going to die? Does that mean the *baby's* going to die? Who is going to die?"

And on every side of the box it's the same thing.

VOICE 1: Warning! Choking hazard!
VOICE 2: Warning! Could cause strangulation!
VOICE 3: Warning! May cause death!

Finally, I say, "If this thing is so dangerous.., Why would someone give it to us?"

My Wife says…, "You have no idea what it's like to be pregnant…"

"Of course I know what it's like to be pregnant," I say. "I'm psychologically pregnant…"

"Then next time *you* carry the baby."

"I might not be the one *carrying* the baby, but I am *also* becoming a parent here, too, you know."

"You're not hearing me," my Wife says. "What's going on with *me…is earth shattering*. I'm huge. My body is completely changed. I can't even walk through our apartment without walking into the walls, and you tell me you're *psychologically pregnant*? What is that? My experience physically is *so overwhelming*, and you're not having that experience."

"But I am *having* an experience."
"What is this a competition?"
"No."
"Are you looking for attention…?"
"No."
"THEN STOP WHINING!"

That night I stay up way too late.

I watch Sunday Night Football.
It's the Green Bay Packers versus the New York Giants.

Flashback.

Fall.
My senior year in high school.
A Monday afternoon.
I come home and my Dad surprises me again. This time with tickets for us to see the Packers versus the Giants on Monday Night Football.
Now I am a massive Green Bay Packers fan…because of my Dad.
And my Dad is a massive Green Bay Packers fan…because of Vince Lombardi.

My Dad *idolized* Vince Lombardi to the point that whenever we were driving on the New Jersey Turnpike he would pull into the Vince Lombardi Service Area simply because it was the Vince Lombardi Service Area.

"Thomas…," he would say. "Vince Lombardi was a *pisan*. Don't ever forget that…"

Rooting with my Dad for the Green Bay Packers was my favorite thing that we shared together.

Now our seats are right on the 50-yard line, but as we sit down, I notice that right behind us is *another* father and his son, but the son is developmentally disabled, and I'm very conscious of them bonding together in the same way that we are. But the game starts, and before you know it it's the end of the first quarter, and my Dad says, "Let's go get my hot dog." My Dad's quota was one hot dog, and two beers at every game.

We get up from our seats, walk through the tunnel, and…there's the father who was sitting behind us.

He's standing *over* his son who is lying collapsed on the stadium's concrete floor.

The father looks around frantically.

"Help me!" he says. "Somebody help me!"

And my Dad does not hesitate.

He goes straight over to the father, looks down at the son; then falls to his knees, and begins to administer mouth-to-mouth resuscitation.

It was one his skills as a fireman.

And as I stand there a ring of people slowly begins to form a circle around my Dad, and without even realizing it I get pushed further and further away until I'm on the outside looking in, peering through the crowd…at my Dad.

Deep into the 8th month of my Wife's pregnancy.

I come home, and find her on her cell phone, but this time she's talking to her OBGYN, telling him about some kind of episode she's had, lights flashing before her eyes.

"In fact…," she says. "I'm having one right now."

"That's a red flag," he says. "I want you to go to the hospital immediately."

We enter St. Luke's through the emergency room, and my Wife is whisked away in a wheelchair.

A little while later, I'm approached by a Nurse.

"Is your Wife the one who has pre-eclampsia?"

"Pre-what?"

"Pre-eclampsia."

"I don't know."

"Is she seeing flashing lights?"

"Yes," I say. "Why didn't you say that in the first place?"

"I'm a nurse," she says. "I'm supposed to use medical terms."

"Is everything okay?"

"No," she says. "The Doctor needs to induce labor."

(We HEAR the SOUND of BEEPS and MONITORS.)

I'm led into a holding room.

I start thinking about my Mother, *my adoptive Mother*, who got pregnant, and nine months later went into labor on the exact day that the doctor predicted. The Baby, a girl, was born with mucus lodged in her throat. The doctors tried to clear the Baby's windpipe, but…they couldn't…and…she died.

I had heard this story many, many times before, but only now does it truly register, only *now* does the horror of that story seem real.

And what about my birth?

What about me?

I was taken from my biological mother immediately after I was born and brought straight to an orphanage.

My adoptive parents by this point had been trying to get pregnant again for *five years*, and when their doctor finally suggested, "If you want a child that badly why don't you adopt?"

They did.

They adopted me.

But that's another story.

I can't have a child.
I don't deserve a child!

And then the doors to the O.R. swing open.

(THOMAS is momentarily blinded by a harsh white LIGHT.)

The O-B-G-Y-N stands waiting.

"Mr. DaGato?"

"Yes."

"Follow me."

(In SLOW MOTION, THOMAS steps toward the LIGHT; then...abruptly, LIGHTS come back up to full.)

Flashback.

Four months earlier.
I come home from teaching, and find my Wife waiting for me at the door.
"We have to move," she says. "This is ridiculous. We're about to have a baby. This is a third floor walk-up. We can't live here anymore."
I say, *"But it's a rent controlled apartment..."*
It's this sweet one-bedroom with a little office right on Washington Street...*a three-minute walk to the PATH train.* And, yes...it does have electric baseboard heat that actually does...well...nothing, and...yes...there's only enough hot water for one shower at a time, but the rent is $750 a month!
My Wife adds, "But there's not enough room for a baby."

Two weeks later.

(We HEAR music, distinctly Italian in flavor.)

My Wife and I are standing in the front courtyard of a three-family house, located in the back of Hoboken that looks like something out of a...Fellini film. It's owned by an Italian couple in their 70s, from Italy, who remind me of my grandparents. They barely speak English, although they do speak well enough to let us know we can rent out the middle floor of their building.
The actual building itself is set back around 30 yards from the sidewalk, and the *piazza* is filled with fountains, fig trees, white marble statuaries – roaring lions, a bust of David, a shrine to the Virgin Mary. And the entire property is surrounded by this six-foot high black metal spiked fence lined with fairy lights.
"What do you think?" my Wife asks.

"I think we'll be safe here," I say. "It's a gated community."

Our realtor – Cosmo Manzoni – turns us on to this independent moving company, run by a group of off-duty firemen, which I look at as a good omen, and we move in.

Now all we needed was the baby.

Back to the present - The hospital.

We name her...Rosie, after the Springsteen song – "Rosalita."

After my Wife and I realize that there's no way we could come up with a name to please all the relatives, we settle on Rosie, because Springsteen's music has meant something to us. Or, as my Wife would say, "It's meant something to you." Because she wasn't completely sold on the idea. "You know what that song is about, right?"

What sold her was a vision I have of our daughter.

She's in her mid-20s.

Spring has sprung and she's driving up a highway somewhere. The windows in the car are open, her hair is blowing in the wind, and "Rosalita" comes on the radio.

Now I am someone who firmly believes that you can hear a song a thousand times before you *really* hear it for the first time. And in my vision, our daughter *has* that moment...and for the first time she hears in Springsteen's music all the freedom and joy and triumph that "Rosalita" represents.

The day we come home from the hospital.

I buy my Wife a pushing present from Tiffany's.

As I stand on the corner waiting for the light to change, a woman sidles up next to me, looks down at the egg-shell blue bag in my hand, and says, "You are a very smart man."

In the car, we strap Rosie into the baby seat using the five-point harness, and my Wife climbs into the backseat with her.

I drive 10 miles an hour all the way back to Hoboken.

To try and cut the tension in the car, I turn on the radio…

VOICE: …and Bruce Springsteen and the E-Street Band will be playing a four-night stand this Spring at Madison Square Garden…tickets go on sale this Saturday.

I turn around to look at my Wife, and she says…, "What? You're not thinking about going are you? *We have a baby now*."

And I don't say a word.

I turn back around, and…I keep driving.

It's the beginning of a great adventure.

There's no time to think about it…it's…*on*.
We bring her home.
We incorporate her into our lives.
She's beautiful.
Her mother's beautiful.

She eats.
She sleeps.
She poops.

The Baby not my Wife.

We go for a visit to MJ's house.

While the wives ohh and ahh over Rosie, he and I steal out to the balcony.

He lives on the 10th floor.

"A daughter...," he says.

(Pause.)

"What?" I say.

"Lemme tell you what my Dad told me about the father-daughter relationship," he says. "There are four stages. The day she's born. The first time she won't hold your hand when you're walking through the mall. The first time she's 10 minutes late for curfew. And on her wedding day...and on her wedding day...you're happy on the outside, but on the inside...you're crying."

"What happens between missing curfew and the wedding...?"

"Trouble, I guess...plenty of trouble."

"And do I get my Dad stripes somewhere in there?"

"You'll get your Dad stripes..., he says." "When an Older Dad gives you his blessings. That is how Dad's get initiated into the world. Older Dad's need to give younger men their Zeus energy."

"Zeus energy?" I ask.

"Yeah, Zeus" he says. "Greek God. Father of men. Lightning bolt in his right hand. You need his energy."

And as I ponder this concept I lean my elbows onto the balcony railing, and I look down...10 ...floors...below.

Flashback.

MJ and I are working at the Plaza Theater where we work practically every day after high school. It's one of the last of the old movie palaces. And we smell our boss - Mr. Kubiak, who we call Stubby K., come through the front door. We always knew when he came in, because he smoked a pipe, and we could smell him long before we saw him.

And Stubby K. says, "You guys need to go up on the roof and clean out the gutters."

And so MJ and I climb up this metal ladder on the side of the movie theatre – five stories high – it's probably the highest point in our town, and there's this beautiful vista up there that stretches all the way out to the New York City skyline.

We clean out the gutters.

MJ goes back down the ladder.

I start to follow, and......I freeze.

I totally freeze.

MJ's like, "What are you doing?"

I say, "I'm not coming down."

"Why not?"

I say, "Because everything is spinning!"

And then MJ runs and gets Stubby K., who comes out and yells, "What's going on up there?"

"I'm not coming down."

He says, "You *gotta* come down."

"*I'm not coming down!*"

And then they both run back inside.

Ten minutes later...I watch as three fire engines – a pumper truck, an aerial ladder truck, and a chief's limo – pull into the parking lot directly behind the theater.

And my Dad climbs out from behind the wheel of the pumper truck.

He sees me...walks straight over to the ladder, and yells up, "THOMAS, YOU GET DOWN HERE RIGHT NOW!!!!"

And whoosh...I go right back down the ladder.

Then my Uncle Stretch, who by this time is a captain, says in a voice loud enough for everyone to hear, "He'll make a great fireman if we start using step ladders!"

Back in Hoboken.

We return to our gated community.
I check our mailbox before entering the building, and I find...a letter of non-renewal from my job.

Now over the course of my life, I had worked in PR, I had worked for an ad firm, and then for a while for a non-profit foundation, but after I met my Wife, she inspired me to go back to school...get a master's degree, and I became a high school history teacher.
But because budget deficits were followed directly by cuts to state funding, I suddenly find myself...without a job.
"We'll figure it out...," My Wife says.

(He starts to take off his dress shirt and tie, reveals a faded Maxwell's rock club t-shirt underneath.)

And we re-think everything.
My Wife has tenure so she has to go back to her teaching job. Forget daycare. That's no longer an option. Not at $2,000 a month. And as for me? We decide that I will be a stay-at-home father.

September.

My Wife goes back to work.
It's my first day on the job.
We're standing on the corner of 3rd and Washington, waiting for the light to change, and an Old Man peers into our stroller, and says, "He's a cute little one."
"*She* sure is...," I say.

And what comes to me immediately is this reality.
It's harder for girls.
Rosie is still in diapers, and she's already fighting for her place in the world, *because* she's a girl.

"Look at how nice he's sleeping."
"*She's* a very good sleeper," I say.
And then the Old Man turns to me. "And now you don't sleep *ever again*. You fathers today all have to do everything. You all have to be Mr. Mom."

MR. MOM…a movie that came out 30 years ago…is about a guy who loses his job, stays at home to take care of his kids, and fails at trying to be a mom. And so here *I* am, trying to earn the right to be called Dad, and on Day One I'm already labeled as an incompetent mom.

But I *am* on the job.
And this is what I find.

It's 50% love fest.
Forty percent backbreaking work.
And 10% utter boredom.

The way she kneads her hands when I give her a bottle…love fest!
How she *refuses* to let me sit down, and/or put her down until she falls asleep…backbreaking!
And then, when she finally *does* wake up, the routine simply repeats itself – feed me, hold me, change my diaper, feed me, hold me, change my diaper.
It's boring!

One morning we're dancing around the living room to Bob Marley, because allegedly reggae replicates the rhythms of the womb, and of course I can't put her down, and my arms are breaking off...

...if you are about to have a child this would be my advice to you. Go to the gym, take a 25-pound plate, make a medallion out of it and wear it for the full-term of the pregnancy. By the time the baby comes you'll be in shape.

...anyway...I dance her up to a mirror so that she can see her reflection, and......I realize that I now have President's hair!
This is me before I got elected...

(He throws back imaginary locks, long and flowing.)

...and this is me now...gone gray...overnight!

The Old Man on the corner was right about one thing...I don't sleep.
I have nightmares *all the time* – Rosie gets hit by a PATH train, she falls into a swimming pool, she gets tossed up and into a ceiling fan.
When my Wife leaves for work in the morning, I can't help but think, I wish *I* were going to work...I wish *I* could stare out my office window...daydream...go out to lunch.
I'd be happy if I could take a shower.
Because staying at home...?
Raising a kid...?
It's twice as hard.

And what's worse...

...I start to get this feeling that I'm doing an awful job.

Now a lot has been written recently about father's taking more of an interest in the raising of their kids, *but* according to the New York Times only 3.4% of the population actually self-identifies as a stay-at-home father.

Mothers, on the other hand, have always gathered and collected – questions, stories – about the experience of being a mother. But men...? We don't have that kind of sounding board, and I'm starting to feel – whether it's true or not – that as a stay-at-home father...I have no idea what I am doing, and that I will *never* earn the right to be called Dad.

In a moment of utter *loneliness*, I give myself over to a group of four Israelis mothers, who live together in a building directly across the street from ours. They adopt me. And at first...I think they invite me in because they all have sons and they love having a little girl around, but what I come to realize is they adopt me because they feel bad for me! We would have lunch out in their backyard, and I would reach into my bag for like some *Saltine crackers*, and by the time I would turn back around, each of the Israelis mom's has gone...WOOSH!...and has thrown out a blanket filled with a full-course meal – *pureed* brisket, cabbage...cooked extra soft...and this seemingly endless supply of apples and honey leftover from Rosh Hashanah... which they would share...and we would sit and feed the kids, and they would talk only to each other...*in Hebrew*...and every now and then one of them would turn to me, and in perfect English say, "It's a shame you don't speak Hebrew."

And so I disentangle myself from them, and off I go...searching for the keys to this mythical title – *Dad*.

On the street I pass other fathers, wearing baby carriers or pushing strollers, and I start looking for the nod; the heads up acknowledgement of our shared fraternity, which I hope will open the door to some further discussion about what the heck it is we're doing.

But I *never* get a response.

Not from a single father.

Either they're too involved with their own child, nervous, or…whatever. But it's like they don't even see me. We walk right past each other.

I stew over this in front of the television where the reminders continue – that fathers are basically idiots, and that we are completely oblivious to our child's needs.

"Recommended by Dr. Mom."

"Choosy mothers choose Jif."

"Kid tested, mother approved."

And a diaper campaign that boasts "The Dad Test" – diapers that are so good, men can use them without help from their wives.

The flipside to this is that the books that have started to accumulate in our daughter's room– WHERE THE WILD THINGS ARE, CAT IN A HAT, GOODNIGHT MOON, etc. – don't mention fathers *at all!*

And so one night…I'm surfing the internet…and, finally, finally…I come across a lifeline: The Hoboken Dad's Group.

I go onto their website, and I find….*nothing*. There's nothing listed on their events calendar. There's a slide show with no pictures, and a resources tab that when clicked on suddenly offers you information in Spanish.

By contrast the Hoboken Mommies Group…has more than 5,000 members.

And so what I decide to do is learn what I need to learn where all the important things in life are learned...on the playground, and I go off to look for other fathers, fathers who I plan to confront head-on about what it is we're doing, except this is what I find: five Jamaican nannies; four moms; and me.

The Jamaican nannies ignore me.

The mom's talk over me as if I am not even there, except when one of their sons gravitates in my direction, going, "Da-da. Da-da," and the mother scoops him up, and says, "He's not your daddy! Your daddy has a job!"

I exit the playground.
A few blocks later, I see this father...pushing a stroller.
He's coming straight towards me.
I give him the nod.

And he doesn't acknowledge me!

So I challenge him, I say, "Hey! How come no greeting?"

"What?"

"I gave you the nod," I say. "How come we didn't stop to talk about what it's like being a Dad?"

"I don't know," he says. "Because I don't feel like a Dad...? I feel like I'm all alone out here."

"Me, too." I say.

My Wife suggests we go out on a date, our first since the baby was born.

She says, "It's important that we get some semblance of our romantic life back."

We go to Lupa in the West Village, order a bottle of wine.

But my *resentment* at being a stay-at-home father has tipped the weight of responsibility into what feels like a total imbalance.

I ask my Wife, "What are *you* feeling? All those hours at work. Being away…"

"Well…," she says. "It's…um…complicated. I feel really happy to be doing what I'm doing."

"Going to work?"

"I feel fortunate to *have* work."

"Because I feel like everything's on me."

"On us," my Wife says. "*I feel grateful that I can pay our bills.*"

And, of course, she's right…no matter how the work load gets divided, we're in this together.

We push on.

Fall.
Christmas.

And then it's February.
Super Bowl Sunday.
And it's my Wife's birthday.
We invite MJ and Christina over to have dinner and watch the game.

My Wife is in the living room breast feeding Rosie.
I'm cleaning the house.
I look at my watch – 4:30. I think.., I have to take a shower. Our dinner guests are going to be here. I go into the bedroom to change, and…

(Smoke slowly begins to fill the stage.)

...I look over at the air conditioner, which lives in the window year-round, and smoke is pouring through the vents.

I race over to look outside, and I immediately know...it's bad. I see people out in the street running around, coming out of their buildings, pointing.

I can hear fire engines in the distance.

I press my face against the window pane, look to my left...and from the building next door I can see flames and black smoke billowing downwind straight towards me.

I turn around, and say, "There's a fire!"

My Wife is like..., "What?"

"I'M SERIOUS!" I say. "There's a fire! Take the baby! We have to get out of here! Right now! Go!"

My Wife unlatches Rosie, grabs their puffy coats, and BAM they're gone.

I grab the strong box from under our bed, scoop my laptop off my desk, and then as I make my way down the stairs, I grab our stroller, which is parked in the hallway, and I muscle it out the door.

I race to meet my Wife who is standing on the sidewalk holding Rosie, and we immediately put her into the stroller; then I turn and sprint back into the building – to the apartment of the old, Italian couple.

I BANG on the door.

There's no answer.

I try the door knob, peer inside.

The grandmother figure stands in the kitchen doorway completely frozen. She can't move. *She cannot move.* I take her arm as gently, but as forcefully as I can, and I say, "I'm sorry...we have to go...c'mon...we have to go...now." And she's like this two-year-old with her heels dug into the ground. She's completely resistant...fighting me every step of the way.

Sobbing!
Wailing!
In Italian!

(He imitates a Woman WAILING…its gibberish, but with an Italian accent.)

And the two of us move in seemingly slow motion through thick black smoke.
I get her to the sidewalk, turn back around, and…watch as flames rise through the roof of the building next door, travel across to our roof…and cut straight down through the center of our building.

Then MJ and Christina show up for dinner carrying two bottles of wine and an appetizer!

We stand there and watch the flames.
One errant cigarette.
Three buildings ablaze.

I turn to a Fireman, and say, "Do you know what make this even worse?"
He says, "That the Super Bowl is on?"
"No," I say. *"Today is my wife's birthday.*
And then I tell him about how the night before my Wife told me that when she was a kid her favorite dessert was the Baskin-Robbins ice cream log cake. And I went on-line to find out where all the Baskin-Robbins locations were in Manhattan, and I spent probably two hours this morning schlepping all over the city trying to find a store that actually had the cake in stock. And when I got home, I went downstairs and I asked the landlord if I could keep the cake in their freezer, because it was going to be a surprise for my Wife's birthday.

And the Fireman hear this…smacks down his mask…walks straight into the fire, comes back out two minutes later, and hands me the cake.

MJ and Christina's apartment…

…my Wife, Rosie and I sleep together on a futon.
We wake to the early morning sound of a clock radio.

VOICE: Futures are down today.

The headlines in the local papers read: Eight Families are displaced by Three-Alarm Fire; Heavy Hearts at Scene of the Blaze.
I send out a mass e-mail to friends and family, and instantly receive back more than 40 responses.

VOICE 1: I'm shocked.
VOICE 2: That's awful.
VOICE 3: What can I do?

That afternoon, wearing only the clothes on our backs, my Wife and I go into Macy's, and buy two suitcases, which we fill only with the essentials we need to live.

I can't believe that our house burned down.

How was I ever going to earn the right to be called Dad when I couldn't provide the most basic of Maslow's needs?
Shelter.
Security.

That night a teacher who works with my Wife drives into Hoboken, and presents us with a cardboard shoebox that had been passed around the school from teachers to students to parents.

    We open the lid and find more than a $1,000 in cash.

    We hold hands, and we cry.

The next morning.

    After another sleepless night…we notice that Rosie isn't breathing right that she's…*wheezing*…and so we take her to her Pediatrician, who wears a white lab coat over a black party dress and heels. My Wife tells the Pediatrician about the fire, and how when she was fleeing, she paused for a moment on the stairs to wait for me, but that the smoke was too thick, and that she quickly continued on.

    The Pediatrician connects Rosie to a monitor; then puts a stethoscope onto her chest and listens. Rosie thinks it's a game, grabs onto the tube, and giggles.

    All of us turn toward the monitor, and there it is…Rosie's heart beating, beating, beating.

    I feel helpless.

    We're sent home with a nebulizer, a loud/scary drug delivery device administered through an oxygen mask that sends medication straight into Rosie's lungs.

    We call it The Torture Machine.

    (We hear the SOUND of a nebulizer, a motorized whirl. THOMAS puts the mask over ROSIE'S face. The machine grows LOUDER and LOUDER until finally – SILENCE.)

And we try to survive.

Over the next three months we live in six different places in Hoboken and New York City.

I shop for a new apartment - *exhaustively*, but find nothing that fits, nothing that we can call home. I go out with realtors in Hoboken on *15 separate occasions*, and it's not like I'm moving fast and free. *I have Rosie with me.*

Finally, I say to this one Realtor, "Please. Don't waste my time. Okay? I can't see another apartment that's meant for college kids. Just because it says two bedrooms doesn't mean it *has* two bedrooms. I'm a grown man with a family. I need a place that we can live in."

The Realtor tells me about this beautiful little place on Washington Street that would be perfect for our family.

We walk over to the building, and as we approach, I say..., "Where are you taking me?"

And I realize that the Realtor is bringing me to see our old, no-longer-rent-controlled former apartment!

I say, "You know what? I'm done. I have to go. I can't see any more places. She has to be feed. I need to change her diaper. I'm done."

I lose 15 pounds.
I grow melancholy.
Then depressed.
And then I'm simply hanging on.
Everything is so intense that I forget everything I need to do two seconds after I say, "You know what I need to do..."

One time, a guy on the street asks me, "Can I get a little help?"

And I tell him, "*I'm homeless.*"

Eventually, I develop a pinched nerve in my neck that becomes unbearable; the pain stretches straight down my arm and into my hand, which feels numb.

I go to see our Doctor, who writes me a prescription for Xanax.

I say, "I don't want it…"

"Take it…," he says. "You need something."

And what's even more important…

…*Rosie* needs something. She's not digging all this lack of security. When we try to put her down she starts screaming, crying for an hour, two hours straight without a break.

One night I ask my Wife, "Do you have a paper clip?"

"A paper clip?" she says. *"Why would I have a paper clip?"* Then she bursts into tears. "Where's the Xanax?" she asks.

MJ takes me out for beers, tries to pick-up my spirits.

"You should be thankful," he says.

"For what?" I say. "We lost everything."

"You didn't *lose* everything," he says. "You still have your Wife. Your daughter. I understand if you're down, but things happen in this world that you can't control. That doesn't make you a bad father. It means you're living in the world. As the saying goes, 'There may be an award for Parents of the Year, but…*no one's ever won it…*'"

We end up at my Mother's house.

The suburbs.
The house I grew up in.
We go there to re-group, recuperate.

And as we pull into the driveway, I say to my Wife, "This is sooo weird. My father was a fireman, and as soon as I *become* a father, my house burns down."

We enter the living room, and...

Flashback.

Winter.
My senior year in high school.

My Dad is holding an application to the fire department...he screams at me, "You got scared on a ladder. So what? They'll stick you on an engine company. You'll work a hose line."
"I don't want to be a fireman."
"And what do *you* wanna do Mr. Big Shot?"
"I want to go to college."
"College...?" my Dad says. "Who from this family ever went to college?"
"Maybe I can be the first?" I say.
"You think you're too good to be a fireman?"
"No."
"Are you ashamed of me?"
"No."
"Because being a fireman is a good job. It's a privilege to be a fireman. Down at that firehouse? We're a family. *It's a good life.* And if it's good enough for me...it's good enough for you."
And then my Dad sticks the application for the fire department into my hands, and says, "You're coming on."

One month later.
My Dad comes back from a house fire, and has a heart attack on his bunk.

Four o'clock in the morning there's a knock at our door. It's my Uncle Stretch, he says…, "Your Dad's dead."

(We HEAR the SOUND of a snare drum, a funeral cadence.)

My Dad's funeral.
I'll sum it up with an image.
His flag-draped coffin rests on the back of a fire truck, paused in front of No. 2 House, and a line of firemen…hundreds long…extends down St. George Avenue, and offers him a final salute goodbye.

(The drums rumble and build; then stop abruptly.)

On the way back from the funeral, we're in a limousine, my Mother is completely out of it and her doctor has written her a prescription. We stop at Shor's Drugs, and I jump out to pick-up the medication, and the Pharmacist says to me, "I'm sorry. But your insurance has been canceled."

We tell Uncle Stretch, and he goes up to City Hall to talk to The Mayor, and then he comes over the house, and tells my Mother, "He's not going to get his pension, either. He died too soon."

My Dad worked the job for 24 years and three months.
But he came up nine months short of vesting.
Meaning…
No health insurance.
No pension.
Nothing.

I re-tell all of this to my Wife as we lie awake in my childhood bed.

She indulges me the way couples do when they've heard each other's stories countless times.

And I tell her about how when I eventually did decide to go to college, how I sold my Dad's 1964 Ludwig, black pearl, Ringo Starr drum kit to help pay for tuition.

"I made the decision at a Springsteen concert," I say. "It was at Madison Square Garden…right after my Dad died, and Bruce played "Independence Day." It's about a son leaving home, and he wants his father to 'just say goodbye.' And listening to it I had this revelation – that with my Dad gone, I was going to need guidance, and so I let Springsteen's music act as a road map, and of course it lead me right back to my own Dad, and how *his* plan was that once he got to the end, he would finally be able to enjoy life. Once he *retired* he could do all the things he really wanted to do, but didn't...and I said to myself..., I am *not* my Dad. I don't want to *become* my Dad. I don't want to *be* a Dad."

"I knew it!" my Wife says.

"Knew what?"

"You never wanted to be a Dad. I knew something was off with you. That's why I kept asking…, 'Are you going to be here for me?' Why didn't you tell me? Why did you agree to have a baby if that's how you felt?"

"Because it was important to you, and because it was important to you it was important to me."

"You should have told me."

"I'm sorry."

"What do we do now?"

Slow Fade To Black

ACT THREE

(LIGHTS rise on THOMAS.)

The next morning I wander down to the cellar.

    In the basement of the house there was a workshop that we called Daddy's Room, and it remained virtually intact since my Dad's death.
    His fire jacket still hung behind the door.
    His tools were still on his work bench.
    The calendar where he X'd off his last days on the job still remained tacked into the wall.
    But then I notice something that I had never seen before…right there on the top shelf…a paperback.
    It's a copy of DR. BENJAMIN SPOCK'S - BABY AND CHILD CARE. The front cover reads, "The most widely recommended handbook for parents ever published." Its first printing sold over 12,000,000 copies.
    I flip through.
    Dr. Spock's BABY AND CHILD CARE is 627 pages long, and a grand total of 13 of those pages are devoted to being a father (although three of those pages are dedicated to fatherless children, and how a mother can make it up to the child).
    And I assume that my Dad must have read those *10 pages*, because they're dog-eared and have pencil marks in the margins.
    Is this how he learned to *become* a Dad?
    He might as well have taken advice from Mr. Spock on STAR TREK!

And then I start to see my Dad more clearly than ever before.

Forget the hero worship I had as a kid.

Forget the blame I put on him, because he didn't understand me.

My Dad was a man.

No more, no less.

A man who wanted to be a father so badly that *he adopted me*.

And now?

I was more than a son.

I was a father, too.

(We HEAR the SOUND of a baby crying.)

Rosie.

It no longer mattered what promises I had made after my Dad died about not wanting "to be a Dad." Rosie was on the scene. And her birth meant that a new generation had taken it's rightly place in the life cycle. That life was indeed finite, and that eventually I was going to die, too.

Dad's die.

But not today.

I come back up the stairs, and tell my Wife, "Pack up. We're going."

On the way out the door, I give my Mother a kiss, and I say, "Thank you."

She says, "For what?"

I say, "For everything. Feeding me, changing my diapers, teaching me how to walk…everything. I love you. Thank you."

And then I pile my little family back into the car, and pointed it towards home.

Back towards Hoboken.

The next day.

    I visit the Hoboken Post Office.
    I open our *PO Box*, rifle through the mail, and find an envelope from our insurance company.
    We *did* have renters insurance, and they send us a check for $25,000.
    The negative part of that equation is that our estimated loss was $43,000.

Flashback.

    Two months *before* the fire.
    We receive our insurance bill; the old fashioned way, by mail. And I write them a check, stick it into a stamped, self-addressed return envelope, and I lick it closed.
    Then, as I always do now when I'm paying our bills, I pour myself a very strong cocktail and I start contemplating the receipt...and I say to my Wife, "You know, our renters insurance only covers $25,000, and now with Rosie we have another whole person in the house, *plus* another room full of things. We should raise our premium to $50,000."
    And my Wife says, "Okay."
    And so across the receipt I write: CALL TO INCREASE. And then I throw the receipt into a fruit bowl where we keep all of our bills.
    "We'll do it next time," I say. "I mean what's the odds of our house burning down between now and then?"

Eventually...I do find us an apartment...

    We move in.
    And on our very first night in the new building.

(The SOUND of a modern fire alarm, flashing LIGHTS. An automated VOICE is heard.)

VOICE: May I have your attention, please. May I have your attention, please. There has been a fire reported on your floor. There has been a fire reported on your floor. Please proceed to the stairways an exit the building. Do not use the elevators. *(Pause.)* May I have your attention, please…

We stop what we're doing.
I grab our strong box, my laptop, my Wife grabs Rosie, and this time we carry the stroller down six…flights…of…stairs.
The fire department arrives, and they head straight into the building; then come right back out again…*false alarm*.

Two hours later.

(The SOUND of a modern fire alarm, flashing LIGHTS.)

VOICE: May I have your attention, please. May I have your attention, please…

This time?
We march down six flights of stairs, go straight into the W-Hotel, and order martinis.

But we're right back on track.

Sort of…
I continue my commitment to being Rosie's father, and my Wife doesn't mention that fact I initially didn't want to be a father.
And so…I do what needs to be done. Every month there's a new first…a new challenge, and on and on it goes, and then suddenly she's a toddler.

And this is what I find.

It's – 70% love.
…and 30% taming a wild animal.

    Picture: The two of us watching MARY POPPINS, which I have seen so many times now that if I ever were to meet Julie Andrews I don't know if I would thank her or kick her in the shins…and Rosie and I are squeezed together into this sickly orange Dora The Explorer couch in the middle of the living room floor, and she's curled into me with her head resting against my chest right over my heart and out of nowhere she leans up, and…she kisses me on the cheek.
Love.
Having to pick her up under my arm kicking and screaming and fighting and having to carry her all the way from Pier A back to the apartment with one arm pushing the stroller and having to stop two or three times to rest because my wrist is breaking and my back is seizing and I am ignoring all on-lookers because my inner voice is screaming, "You're a bad parent! You're a bad parent!" Yet focusing on the mission at hand…*to get her home*…because, "It's time to leave means it's time to leave!"
That's taming a wild animal.
It's fun being a parent.

Early Monday morning – Spring.

(We HEAR the SOUND of fire engines, off in the distance. THOMAS listens intently as the sound grows closer and closer; then passes…FADES.)

    Every time I hear the sound of fire engines now my back goes up.

This time the fire trucks drive right past the front of our building.

And since there's no going back to sleep, and the sun is already shining, I simply pack Rosie into the stroller, and off we go…for a walk. Now maybe it was an accident…maybe I did it on purpose, maybe I did subconsciously. I don't know. But I make one quick turn, and suddenly we're on our old block, outside our old house, which is now nothing more than a demolition site. A chain-link fence has been erected temporarily around the property, and all that remains on the other side is a chest-high pile of rubble.

Wood, plaster, brick, and ash, ash……ashes.
We all fall down.

I look into Rosie eyes, and I think, "She won't remember any of this…"

And then just as quickly I find myself walking away, trying to put it all behind me.

There's this smell like smoked sausages that lingers on my clothes.

I feel like I need a shower.
I push Rosie faster and faster, away, uphill.
Where to?
I don't know.
The Dolphin Park.
The Mud Pit at Fantasy Island.

We end up at Privacy Park – Elysian – where my Wife use to go to breastfeed, and I wheel Rosie over to a plot of grass that looks out on the Empire State Building. I lift her out of the stroller, reach into my bag, and…WOOSH!…throw out a blanket filled with a full-course meal – diced chicken, broccoli…cooked extra soft…and a seemingly endless supply of apples and honey bought at the 24-hour bodega.

But by the time I turn back around Rosie has already waddled off to this little fountain and she stomps right into the water and her face lights up.

And me?

I kick off my "mandals"...as my Wife likes to call them...and I follow right after her, into the water...and we let it wash over us.

When we get back to our blanket I realize that someone has been watching us...a couple...sitting maybe 20-feet away on a bench. They're holding hands. And the Woman is clearly *very* pregnant and she turns to the Man, and she says in a sing-song voice..., "That's going to be you soon."

And I smile.

And I give the Man the nod.

And he nods back.

Father's Day.

My Wife wakes me up with a question, "Is Father's Day supposed to *mean* something?"

"It means it's the least recognized day in the United States," I say.

But on the kitchen table I find a card "from my daughter" labeled: To His Fatherness. And when I open it...I find two tickets inside to see Bruce Springsteen & the E-Street Band at Madison Square Garden.

"For you," My Wife says. "You earned it....we're going to see Bruce."

The show, which is completely sold out...is that very night...and I put on one of my favorite bootlegs – Live in Winterland, San Francisco – and the two of us start to get really, really excited, grooving around the house to "Prove It All Night" with The Professor Roy Bittan's extended piano jam intro.

And then my Mother shows up to babysit…, "Happy Father's Day!"

And off we go to Madison Square Garden.

We enter the arena, and stomp happily down these metal grandstand-esque stairs at the back of the floor, searching for our seats, checking row numbers; then double checking the seats listed on our tickets until finally we……find our seats; then we…*triple check* the numbers listed on our tickets.

Our seats are directly behind the sound board.

We are literally looking into the ass crack of the sound engineer.

My Wife goes, "Oh, my God. I don't even want to tell you how much I paid for these tickets. I got ripped off…I got totally ripped off…"

"It's okay," I say.

"No. It's not okay."

"Hey…," I say. "…at least we're on a date."

"This is supposed to be a thank you present!"

"For what?"

"For doing all you've done as a father."

"I don't know what I'm doing."

"Yes! You do!" she says. *"You've been doing it all along."*

And then abruptly, I feel this tap on my shoulder.

I look up, and…an Usher, and a Security Guard are standing over us.

The Usher asks, "Could I see your tickets?"

I'm thinking, "Now what?" And I hand him our tickets.

"What are they counterfeit?" I ask.

He looks at the tickets, he looks at us, and says, "I'm sorry. You have to come with me."

My Wife and I we…both stand, and…follow the Usher, who leads the way with the Security Guard pulling up the rear.

The Usher leads us around a blue metal barrier, and starts toward the tunnel, toward the exit…my Wife lets out what sounds like the squeek of a wounded animal. *(He imitates.)* But then…just as we're about to slip out of the arena…we suddenly take a hard right turn around another barrier, and we start towards the front of the house.

I begin reading off the letters on the sides of the rows – D, C, B…A.

First row orchestra.

"I'm sorry about the inconvenience," the Usher says. "Those were obviously obstructed vision seats." *(He initials the tickets with a black marker, hands them back; then points toward the center of Row A)*. "Those are your new seats."

I say…, "Is this a joke?"

"It's a ticket upgrade," he says. "Enjoy the show."

My Wife and I do this excuse me, pardon me, shuffle all the way down the row, and then we plop down…into our new seats.

"What…just…happened?" I ask.

My Wife says, "I desperately have to take a pee, but I am NOT LEAVING THESE SEATS! OH, MY GOD! WE'RE HERE!"

"We're here!" I say. "I'm here. I'm here…"

And we embrace.

And in that *exact instant* the lights go off and the show begins.

And *33 songs later*, Springsteen holds up his guitar in his right hand like Zeus with his lightning bolt and he says, "Are there any Mom's and Dad's out there tonight?"

And my Wife and I both raise our hands.

"Well you better call up the babysitter and tell 'em you're gonna be late!" Springsteen says. "'Cause I got one more fairy tale left to sing."
And he plays…, "Rosalita."

                                                             Blackout

END OF PLAY

AFTERWARD

I always get asked the same question after my plays.
"Did _____ really happen?"
And I'm not sure what to say.
How do you explain semi-autobiographical fiction?
It wasn't always that way.

In the beginning of my development as a solo performer, I was deeply influenced by the work of Spalding Gray, whose style was to tell stories directly from his life. Gray, whom I met while working at the Prince Street Bar, which was down the street from the Performing Garage, told me that the only liberty he took with his stories was to occasionally re-structure the timeline of events to increase the drama.

And so I worked the way Gray worked.

I wrote in the first person, I told the truth (my version of it, anyway). And I was spared the question, "Did _____ really happen?" Following Gray's lead, my first two solo works *Whizzy* and *The Jealousy Piece*, both of which premiered in the American Living Room festival at HERE (shout-out to Kristin Marting), were true stories drawn directly from my life.

Then came *My Italy Story*, which was basically a dinner party story I told to friends about a trip I took to Italy, and all that had occurred: family conflicts; ghostly visitations; reuniting with my beloved Cousin Louie, etc., etc. And like my Mother before me the tale got better and better with each telling, until suddenly I realized that this was my next show!

It debuted out-of-town at Penguin Rep, with me playing *me* under Joe Brancato's insightful direction. And since reviews for the play were for the most part positive, I had no reason to believe that my first person style of working wasn't well …working. No one asked, "Did _____ really happen?"

That first iteration of *My Italy Story* had a raw honesty that left little doubt about what *did* happen. And I was also certain about what would happen next - an Off-Broadway producer would move the play into New York.

Except that *didn't* happen…nothing happened.

And everyone involved with the production moved on.

For me, moving on meant going back to Europe, and seeing the countries I had missed the first time around. And with my good friend and travel buddy Michael O'Brien, I started to make plans. Backpacking gear was purchased. Eurorail tickets. We set a departure date, and then…

…TheatreWorks in Hartford called.

They had heard good things about the play, and wanted to add it to the end of their season (remember: this was back in the Nineties, when solo shows were still rare, and the idea of adding one to your season, because it was cheap and easy to do was still a novel idea), which left me with a dilemma.

Should I do the play?

Or should I go to Europe?

So I came up with a solution…, Why not get another actor to play *me*?

And since no one blinked, we held auditions in New York, found the great Danny Mastrogiorgio, who had just graduated from the Juilliard School (although here's an interesting tidbit from my notes on another actor: "Bobby Cannavale – Naked Angels product. Soon to be a Dad. Good instincts. No experience."), and off I went to Europe.

With a week left in the run, I returned, and went straight up to Hartford, where I sat in the back of the house like a good playwright should, and watched Danny play *me* (apologies here for talking about myself in the third person).

From that experience I learned two important things: 1) I was lucky that no one from my family had seen these out-of-town runs or they might have killed me; 2) Real life does not play out in three perfect acts. The experience of watching it through taught me that the play was not as good as it could be, because I remained *too beholden* to the truth.

And so I changed the facts, created a fictional character – Thomas DaGato (who could be played by any actor, including *me*) – combined other characters to create new ones (ones who wouldn't beat me up after the show), and, most importantly, *made-up scenes that did not happen*, all in the name of telling the best story possible. In the process, I found both my voice, *and* my genre of choice – semi-autobiographical fiction – which claims the authority of fact, and the freedom of fiction at the same time.

And, yes…years later…my wife did become pregnant…I did become a stay-at-home dad, and my house did burn to the ground for those who must know. But when I sat down to write *Long Gone Daddy*, I realized this was another story for Thomas DaGato. He could tell this tale way better than I could.

So, as for the question…, "Did _____ really happen?"

The answer is maybe it's best to simply go along for the ride.

No questions asked.

Joseph Gallo
May 2016
Hoboken, NJ

My Italy Story written at 114 Washington Street, #3
Long Gone Daddy written at 235 Hudson Street, #612

www.ingramcontent.com/pod-product-compliance
Lightning Source LLC
Chambersburg PA
CBHW030001050426
42451CB00006B/83